FINDING YOUR RHYTHM

FINDING YOUR RHYTHM

A Five-Step Approach for Creating the Life You Desire

KAREL BAKKES

AUTHENTES
PUBLISHING

Published by Karel Bakkes
authentes.com

Edited and designed by Girl Friday Productions
www.girlfridayproductions.com

Cover design: Bradford Foltz
Interior design: Paul Barrett
Project management: Katherine Richards
Editorial: Bethany Davis

ISBN (paperback): 978-616-588-106-7
ISBN (e-book): 978-616-586-851-8
First edition

To my teachers, who have trusted me with their valuable wisdom.

CONTENTS

FOREWORD

People often come to me for advice because they want to do better, to feel better, to accomplish more, and to struggle less. They have aspirations to climb a mountain of greatness but can't seem to elevate themselves from the plateau they're stuck on. This stagnant feeling is the reason so many of us are unhappy and seemingly unable to make bigger strides upward. We sense something is wrong but can't seem to pinpoint the source. Or if we do happen to make a positive change, it winds up being short-lived. Dissatisfaction in our personal and professional lives is high.

So what is missing?

After working with the world's top executive talent for more than a decade, my answer remains fairly straightforward: to be our best selves, we must develop a strong inner-core capability, a strong outer-core capability, and the ability to execute both in tandem out in the world.

This model is all about balance. We must commit to look inside ourselves at who we really are, hone our exterior abilities, and then be able to marry the two while contributing meaningfully to our communities, whether at home or work. Unfortunately, many of us are markedly off-balance. And guess what is most often the weakest of the trio?

The inner core.

Of these three interdependent facets, the inner core is the most important, yet it's also typically the least developed.

Your inner core comprises the set of characteristics that make you who you are: your values, thoughts, beliefs, emotions, references, and behavioral tendencies. Without evaluating these internal compasses, you risk staying on a plateau forever. Without appraising your inner metrics, you may never find your true purpose in life; you may never reach your full potential.

And there's where this book comes in.

Written by a fellow executive leadership coach who understands the deep significance of accessing the inner core, *Finding Your Rhythm: A Five-Step Approach for Creating the Life You Desire* is designed to help you build self-awareness and harness your inherent gifts so that you can ultimately make authentic choices aligned with your values.

The truth is, many people's innermost character remains an unexplored territory, and this is a shame. Knowing yourself deeply and honestly is actually the key to unlocking your potential. How you think, what you feel, and the values you hold are what drive your best decisions and deepen your connections to others and the activities you love to do.

Yet self-awareness isn't easy for many of us. We are made complacent by what we think we *should* believe or feel, and we build an entire identity around beliefs and values that don't match up with what's actually inside our souls. It's time to change that. If you are looking for a way off the plateau and into a more invigorating environment, this book is for you.

Karel Bakkes's five steps to finding your rhythm teaches us how to break free of identity traps and discover what really makes us tick. In this book, he invites us to examine our limiting beliefs, explore our life's unique purpose, align decisions with our values, and let go of our egos. Through results-driven exercises, Bakkes challenges us to swap negative habits for positive ones and open our self-awareness through mindfulness.

In Step 1, Bakkes guides us to becoming self-aware, which is foundational to all of our pursuits. Self-awareness is the ability to see ourselves clearly and objectively. With awareness of self, we can thoroughly understand our emotional and behavioral reactions to internal and external stimuli. Bakkes lists several ways we can begin to home in on being more observant, from meditation to making music.

In Step 2, we're shown how to listen to what our body is telling us. Our body, mind, and spirit offer a lot of clues to what we need for well-being—we just have tune in. This chapter looks at how to balance the eight dimensions of wellness. It also invites us to examine our values and beliefs through reflective exercises. Because we cannot make sound decisions unless they are in alignment with our own values, this is a particularly important chapter for self-development.

Finding your purpose is what Step 3 is all about. Getting clarity on your purpose is a worthy pursuit because without it you can't be your true self. Without a clear vision of what you are meant to do in this world, you can't share your talents or be part of something bigger than just yourself. This step takes time, effort, and patience. But Bakkes offers tools to make the process doable.

Step 4 challenges us to examine our habits: the ones that we engage in mindlessly, the ones that are damaging, and the helpful ones that we need to start doing more often. Bakkes has combed the latest research in brain and behavioral sciences to offer a distillation of what's been proven to make lasting, positive habit change. Bakkes argues that changing up our habitual patterns—our rhythm—from time to time can boost creativity; likewise, staying stuck in a pattern that's not aligned with our inner core can make us unhappy, even unwell.

Finally, Step 5 of the finding your rhythm journey is where we move into action. Bakkes walks us through creating and executing an action plan to meet new goals. This chapter also addresses bumps along the way, such as how to deal with limiting beliefs that are holding us back. This chapter concludes with how to celebrate achievements both big and small along the way, which is important to keeping us motivated.

Whether you are a currently a leader of others, a future leader, or just wanting to take the lead in your own life, you must look inside. But beware, this is not a once-and-done thing; it's a constant recalibration.

Finding Your Rhythm will help you assess your strengths, showcase the vibrancy of your character, act within your own value system, change negative thinking patterns, and manage your emotional makeup. You'll learn to be more creative, capable of making better decisions, effective at communicating, and able to build meaningful relationships. Most of all, you'll have the skills to be your best, authentic self.

Now and in challenging moments in your future, let this book be your guide to finding your ultimate, unique rhythm.

John Mattone
Bestselling author, premier executive coach
August 2021

ACKNOWLEDGMENTS

Thank you, Nhu Nhu, my loving partner in life, for supporting me every step of the way. Your encouragement was instrumental in getting this book over the finish line; I could not have done it without you. I am so glad we are on this journey together, and I look forward to seeing where it will take us next!

Thank you to my parents for teaching me to never give up and to always look at the positive side of life. I hope this is also, in some way, the book my father always wanted to write during the time he was on this planet.

Thank you to my sons, Guido, Jason, Ryan, and Mason. When I mention "teachers" on the dedication page, you guys are definitely among them. I have learned so much from all of you and hope I can continue doing so for a long time.

Thank you to the Bangkok Capitol Toastmasters Club. You are awesome. Not only did I find out what true love really means through my participation in Toastmasters, but I also got an excellent opportunity to talk about and get feedback on some of the concepts I have included in my book. Go Cappies!

Thank you to Peggy-Jane, who was with me for part of my journey. The work we did together with the Remarkable Foundation was an important starting point for my transformation process.

Thank you to David Bloch, who was at the beginning of my transformational journey fifteen years ago. You helped me open my mind to other perspectives and experiences. I could not have written this book without having you at the start of that journey.

Thank you to my clients, who trusted me to partner with them to solve the challenges they are facing or capture the opportunities ahead of them.

Thank you to Marisa Solís, who coached me during the writing phase. You helped me put more structure to my thinking, and your developmental editing turned the manuscript into one that I was proud to hand over to the publishing company.

Finally, thank you to the team at Girl Friday Productions, who did an amazing job turning my manuscript into the finished book that it is today. You helped me make my dream come true!

FINDING YOUR RHYTHM

At least half the people I've spoken to over the past few years are unhappy in their jobs or are stuck in unhappy relationships. Or both. According to the *World Happiness Report 2021*,[1] there has been a significant increase in overall sadness and worry globally.

Where are you? Are you happy with the work you are doing? Are you satisfied with your relationship? What is your overall happiness score?

Me? I've certainly felt stuck. There was a time when I had the money, I had the house, I had the perfect family. People used to tell me that I had it all. But I did not feel alive; I had no energy. I felt like I was seeing everything in permanent shades of gray. My life was colorless. I felt like I was making my way through a puddle of mud every day. Feeling stuck was wearing me out.

This "stuck" feeling did not make me a very nice person to be around, and as a result I was getting more and more disconnected from the joy I used to experience with my family, my friends, and my work colleagues. I felt disconnected even from myself.

How did this happen? To get more clarity and turn my life around, I started looking for answers. I read self-help books and talked to friends. A few of them suggested that I spend time with a coach and mentioned a specific name: David Bloch. I'd participated in a presentation skills workshop that David led a few years earlier, but I had not thought about him since. However, after three people independently recommended him to me, I decided to reach out to him. After one phone call, I decided to spend a week with him in Denmark. That week would turn out to be transformational for me, the start of a journey that continues today.

One night when I was in Denmark on my coaching retreat with David, I had a very clear dream. It started with me walking down a mountain. There were trees all around me, and they were bending toward me, making everything dark. I felt the sky pressing down on me too. I was very tense and did not notice anything around me because I was on the phone, in a heated discussion. I kept walking.

At the bottom of the mountain, the path I was on rounded into a curve. I could not see where the path was leading, but I did notice a young boy, probably ten to twelve years old, sitting on a bench at the point where the path curved away. I turned off my phone and walked over to him. He was reading a book. When I looked more closely, I realized the boy was actually me when I was around that age! I asked him what book he was reading, and he lifted it up and showed me the pages. They were all blank. He said, "For many years you have had other people write your story. These pages are your life. It is time for you to start writing your own story."

Immediately the darkness disappeared and I felt light and relaxed— and excited! It was a beautiful dream with profound messages that I revisit often. It taught me something that I am passing on to you in these pages: Don't let anyone write your story. Be the author of your own book.

Find your own meaning in life—your own purpose. Don't let other people tell you who you are. Own your story. It took me many years after that dream to fully embrace its message. But here I am, writing my own book!

This book is my gift to you, dear reader.

Here I will share with you all the lessons I have learned through both my personal life experiences and professional coaching sessions with my clients. This book contains the blood, sweat, and many tears that were shed on the journey. In my work, I help individuals reject the status quo of living a life they don't really want. I help them build a life completely aligned with who they are.

As I do with my clients, I will share with you evidenced-based strategies that can get you unstuck, raise your happiness rating, improve your relationships, and deepen your connection to yourself. With my five-step approach to finding your rhythm, you will learn how to . . .

- become more aware through meditation, journaling, spending time in nature, and other mindful activities.
- dial in to whole-body health, which includes emotional, mental, physical, and spiritual wellness.
- find your life's purpose through specially designed exercises.
- ditch habits that no longer serve you, and create new ones based on your values.
- tell—and live—a new story of who you truly are.

My promise to you is that when you get to the end of this book, you will clearly understand the concrete actions you can take to start living the life you desire.

HOW THIS BOOK CAME TOGETHER

Sitting on a plane from Bali to Bangkok just before the Covid-19 pandemic started, I was deep in thought about my goals for 2020. Moving from half sleep to being awake, I suddenly heard myself saying, *I need to find my rhythm.* That message resonated with me—and ignited the birth of this book.

I have always been fascinated by rhythm and music. People say that music is the art form that brings us closest to the gods, and I believe that is true. Music is such a powerful way of communicating. The phrase *finding your rhythm* resonated with me because I immediately felt a connection between the power of rhythm and my passion to help my clients excel in their lives and push their limits. I thought about how listening to a 175-beats-per-minute playlist on my headphones helped me run longer distances. Or how having a certain rhythm in my morning routine helped me get ready for an action-packed day. The more I thought about it, the more questions popped into my head:

- *If people feel stuck, is there a link to a lack of "rhythm" in their lives?*
- *Are there life lessons we can learn from how we experience rhythm?*
- *Is there a link between rhythm and what's happening in our brain?*
- *How can we play with our life rhythm to increase our happiness?*
- *Does rhythm have to be constant to feel good?*
- *How does our individual rhythm interplay with the rhythm of our environment?*

This book explores these questions. Using rhythm as a framework, it examines how we can craft desired changes in our lives. How we can become our authentic selves.

There is so much we can learn from rhythm. We all know that when we hear certain rhythms, we want to start moving. This is the kind of rhythm you want to create in your life—one that gets you moving. But we also know that the same rhythm can become boring over time. Your rhythm will need to change from time to time to keep you moving, growing, thriving.

In this book we will explore how a change to your rhythm can make a world of difference. In just five steps, you can change your rhythm and discover how to live an authentic life—one that is fully aligned with who you truly are.

WHAT IS RHYTHM?

Based on the *Webster's Revised Unabridged Dictionary*,[2] the word *rhythm* can be defined as follows:

- In the widest sense, a dividing into short portions by a regular succession of motions, impulses, sounds, accents, etc., producing an agreeable effect, as in music poetry, the dance, or the like.
- *(Mus.)* Movement in musical time, with periodical recurrence of accent; the measured beat or pulse which marks the character and expression of the music; symmetry of movement and accent. *Moore (Encyc.)*
- A division of lines into short portions by a regular succession of *arses* and *theses*, or percussions and remissions of voice on words or syllables.
- The harmonious flow of vocal sounds.

There are a lot of elements in these definitions that we can recognize in our own lives, especially regarding patterns, movement, and predictability.

Rhythm Is Pattern

Our lives typically have strong behavioral patterns. Beginning in infancy, our brain starts to form billions of connections and create **mind maps**. These mind maps become our navigation devices. As soon as we are faced with something new, we seek out an existing map to guide us through the situation. For example, if our stomach rumbles, we unconsciously place the rumbling on a map that navigates us toward something to eat. Most of the time, this process happens almost automatically, at the subconscious level.

We also create mind maps based on certain behavioral patterns that we have formed by living our day-to-day lives—our morning and bedtime routines, for example—and maps that help us handle certain situations without too much forethought. The same is true for how we react to anger and how we deal with people who challenge us or who are very nice to us. These reactions turn into our behavioral patterns.

Rhythm Is Movement

Our lives have movement, although interestingly, we hardly notice it. We do not see ourselves aging. We look in the mirror and see ourselves just as we are. But with every passing second, we age a little bit more.

Some time ago I saw a YouTube video that was created by compiling photos of the same child taken once a month in the same spot for eighteen years. Videos like that make it easy to see that our lives consist of ongoing movement. Our bodies change as we grow from newborn to toddler, to teenager, to young adult, to older adult. In a similar way, we grow as individuals. Just as nature has seasons, we also have seasons in our lives, such as being single, being married, and having children. There are also more complicated or difficult seasons, such as moving to another country, getting divorced, or losing a loved one. All these changes have a certain movement.

Rhythm Is Predictable

Another important element of rhythm is predictability. Humans are the only species that can predict or anticipate audible rhythms. If I put a metronome in front of you and asked you to tap along with it, you would probably find the rhythm pretty quickly. In a study of chimpanzees, researchers found that they too had a sense of rhythm, but predicting rhythm and tapping along was not something they could do.[3] After a long period of training (one to two years), the chimpanzees were able to come close to the beat, but they were following rather than anticipating it. If a rhythm is not predictable, most people find it difficult, even anxiety provoking, to listen to.

In an experiment with a group of toddlers, researchers put percussion instruments in a room and had the children select the instruments they wanted to play. They did not give any further instructions. As you can imagine, within a short time all the children were making sounds with their instruments, with no coordination. However, within five to ten minutes of beginning the experiment, the children started syncing their rhythms, following the child who was playing the most dominant beat or sound.

Because we automatically predict the pattern of rhythmic sounds, we tend to follow the rhythm of whatever environment we are in. So it's important to realize that the rhythm we are following isn't always the rhythm we actually want to be following!

If you like to play a smooth jazz beat but everyone around you is banging their heads to punk rock, you probably won't feel like you're in the right place. In short, that's what *Finding Your Rhythm* is all about: recognizing the rhythm that you are playing, finding out which rhythm you would like to play, and starting the process of changing your rhythm to be fully in sync with who you want to be.

WHERE DOES RHYTHM COME FROM?

The interesting thing about rhythm is that it's everywhere. When babies are still in their mother's womb, they hear the rhythm of her heartbeat. There is rhythm in our breathing, in the way we walk, in the way we talk. Rhythm is in music, in the sound of an engine, in a train riding on its tracks, in a woodpecker drumming against the trees. Once you start thinking about it, *rhythm is everywhere!*

Where did rhythm come from? Joseph Jordania, an Australian-Georgian ethnomusicologist, evolutionary musicologist, and professor, explained how humans' sense of rhythm developed in the early stages of our evolution.[4] In his research paper "Time to Fight and Time to Relax: Singing and Humming at the Beginnings of Human Evolutionary History," he notes that humans are the only singing species on the ground; all the others live in the water or in trees. So why did humans begin to sing and make rhythmic sounds? It has everything to do with the threat of being eaten alive.

Let's look at birds. A lightweight bird sitting on a thin branch can sing as loudly as it likes without fear of being eaten, since the predators that are the biggest threat to it are on the ground and can't reach it. Have you ever noticed that a bird stops singing when it's on the ground? Now you know why! Of the forty-five hundred singing species on our planet, most live in the trees. Some live in the water. Only one lives on the ground. That one species is us. Humans.

So how did humans survive as the only ground-dwelling singing species? Our ancestors knew that if they made sound, they would be an easy catch for the many predators out there. To protect themselves, they started using loud, rhythmic singing and shouting accompanied by vigorous, threatening body movements. They figured out that when they all did this together, they scared away saber-toothed cats on the lookout for an evening meal.

In order to sound loud and threatening, there was one more thing that our ancestors had to do: coordinate their sounds. So they created rhythmic unity. Unlike the rhythm of most other species, human rhythm is precise. Our ancestors figured out that if they made sound together, exactly at the same time, it would be much louder. What's more, a precise rhythm sends a message to predators about the group's unity and determination to fight. And looking at it from another perspective, making this precise rhythm creates a strong bond among the members of the group.

In addition to using their hands and bodies to create rhythmic sounds, our forebears also used sticks, stones, bones, and anything else they could find that would make a sound when banged against another object. This was how musical instruments developed. From this, drums evolved. Historians are able to trace the first use of drums to 6000 BC. They were basically big holes in the ground with animal skins stretched across them. Our ancestors would hit them with wooden sticks to communicate with others and warn them of approaching danger. The drums also had ceremonial, sacred, and symbolic associations.

These first drums were said to be found in Mesopotamia (in what we now call western Asia), where they were played almost entirely by women. It's said that in the prevailing religious culture in Mesopotamia at the time, the goddess Inanna was thought to have created the drum, and the first drummer was a priestess named Lipushiau. In Egypt, long drums were mainly used by marching soldiers.

China has the longest history of producing cymbals—round plates made of various alloys and used as percussion instruments. During the time of the Silk Road, when people traveled that trading route from China to the Mediterranean Sea, they would bring their musical instruments with them. Trade along the Silk Road led to the spread and evolution of instruments there.

The basic rhythm of traditional music varies by country and region. Because we get used to the rhythm of the environment into which we are born, we sometimes struggle to find the pattern in music from another region. For example, if a rhythm from a West African country were played for British people, they would likely struggle to follow along. And, to be fair, the same can likely be said for most Western people, who would probably struggle to follow or dance to rhythms from outside their own spheres. Why? Because in African countries, music typically plays a much bigger role in daily life than it does in Western countries.[5] For example, in most Western music, there is a clear distinction between the "artist" and the audience, while African music tends to be much more communal. In traditional African music, the audience is not separated from the artists. Everyone participates. Some people play the musical instruments, and other people sing, clap, or dance, but they all join in.

A Fanti drummer once told me that Fanti musicians are guided by what they call a "hidden" rhythm. That's what influences music makers and compels them to create variations around it. As a result, African music can have two, three, or sometimes even four rhythms going on at the same time. Western music, in contrast, has only one rhythm, one beat.

Throughout history and around the world, there has been a strong correlation between certain rhythms and the type of work people do, the physical environment they live in, the sounds around them, and the language they speak. When people have to perform very repetitive tasks or movements for work or are subject to rhythmic sounds (as from machines), they may sing, clap, or stomp along with the movements they make as they work and the sounds they are exposed to. For example, rhythmic songs are used in agriculture to coordinate the movements of the people doing the sowing and harvesting. The music also increases productivity and makes the work more stimulating. Work songs have been developed for many different occupations.[6]

Rhythmic songs were also used by enslaved people. Not only would the rhythms help them perform repetitive tasks, energize them, and make their work more bearable, but the songs also enabled them to communicate messages to one another—messages about frustrations, anger, hopes, and dreams.

A modern example of how sound can be converted into rhythm is found in the song "Lust for Life" by Iggy Pop, the American musician, record producer, and actor who is often called "the Godfather of Punk."[7] In 1977, Iggy Pop was living in Berlin and writing a lot of songs with David Bowie. One evening they were listening to the radio when they heard the Morse code rhythm that was the opening to the American Forces Network news. Bowie picked up his ukulele and started mimicking the rhythm. That was the starting point for "Lust for Life," which became a big hit for Iggy Pop during the punk rock era.

Researchers have found that musical development is strongly related to how cultures developed. Patrick E. Savage, an associate professor at Keio University, in Japan, notes that cultural evolution was foundational to the academic fields of musicology and comparative musicology.[8] One example of the link between a culture and music comes from the Maori, the indigenous inhabitants of New Zealand.

The Maori have a ceremonial dance or challenge called the haka, which is performed by a group and combines rhythmic sounds and movements, such as stomping. The haka was performed by male warriors as a preparation for battle and by both men and women as a dance for various ceremonies.

The haka plays an important role in modern New Zealand culture too. It is still performed to welcome distinguished guests or to mark achievements, special occasions, or funerals. The rest of the world was exposed to the haka when the New Zealand rugby team, the All Blacks, started performing it before their games.

While rhythm can be easily found in cultural ceremonial events, it's also ubiquitous in everyday life. If everything has rhythm, so do our lives—whether it is a daily, weekly, monthly, annual, or even lifelong rhythm. For example, your daily rhythm might be that you get up at 6:00 a.m., exercise, take a shower, eat breakfast, go to work, break for lunch, go back to work, have dinner, read a book and . . . repeat. Your weekly rhythm could be five days of working and two days of weekend. This rhythm that you have created for yourself is your *personal* rhythm: the soundtrack of your life.

If rhythm is the soundtrack of your life, you need to make sure that your environment is in sync with your personal rhythm. If your surroundings and your rhythm are not aligned, you must decide whether you are open to understanding the rhythm around you or if you need to find an environment that better matches your beat.

HOW DOES RHYTHM MAKE YOU MOVE?

To understand how rhythm makes you move, let's look at a group of people for whom moving or initiating movement is difficult: those with Parkinson's disease, a disorder of the central nervous system that affects the motor cortex.

The motor cortex, the part of the brain that makes us move, is found in the brain's frontal lobe and is divided into two major regions— the primary and nonprimary motor cortices. When the primary motor cortex is stimulated, it sends signals to specific muscles in the body to initiate movement. The nonprimary motor cortex coordinates and plans this movement.

In 1870, physicians Gustav Theodor Fritch and Eduard Hitzig researched how this part of the brain functions. Using live dogs, they cut away half their skulls to expose the motor cortex. When they stimulated it through electricity, the dogs moved accordingly.

Parkinson's disease is caused by a decrease in or loss of nerve cells in a part of the brain that produces dopamine, a chemical that is crucial to motor cortex function and that allows brain cells to communicate with each other.

In addition to causing Parkinson's disease, a decrease in dopamine levels can cause many other neurological and psychiatric disorders. Although there is still a lot we don't know about dopamine, significant progress has been made in understanding its role in Parkinson's disease, opening the door to new treatment possibilities.

Research on the impact of rhythm on Parkinson's disease has given us insight.[9] Some of the patients in these studies could barely walk, but when researchers started playing a rhythm, stimulating the part of the brain that activates motor function, the patients were able to walk again.

In an Italian study published in 2016,[10] twenty-six people with Parkinson's disease were selected to participate in a five-month program that included taking a daily twenty-minute walk on a flat surface while listening to rhythmic auditory cues through headphones. The beats per minute were individualized for each patient based on initial measurements of cadence, stride length, and speed. The results were very promising: all the patients showed increased walking speed, improved ability to stabilize cadence, and improved stride length.

If rhythm has such a profound impact on our brains and our ability to operate as human beings, can we use it to our advantage? Can we create a personal rhythm to help us perform at peak levels? Can we find a rhythm that makes us feel happy and fully alive?

Yes we can! By understanding a bit more about how the brain operates, and how what we do enforces patterns (rhythms) in our lives, we can let go of thoughts and behaviors that keep us stuck, bored, and unfulfilled—and establish new habits and rhythms that help us feel energized, emboldened, and satisfied.

WHY ARE RHYTHMIC PATTERNS SO IMPORTANT TO YOUR HEALTH?

If rhythmic music literally gets you moving, it's not a stretch to see how rhythmic patterns literally keep you habituated. This is great if you have healthy habits. But if your habits are making you feel stuck and unsatisfied, you need to introduce new activities to give your brain variety.

Let's return our attention to the brain, which has billions of neurons. As we get older, the speed at which these neurons form new connections and pathways decreases, but the process never stops. The brain continues to change our whole lives—and luckily so. If we didn't have the ability to further develop our brain after a certain age, we would be doomed to live life in a very repetitive way until we leave this planet. But since our brain can continue developing, we can change destructive patterns we get tied up in, we can change our beliefs, and we can learn new things. We can keep growing as human beings! In order to have a healthy, active brain, we need to take care of it—and there are a lot of ways we can do that. Let's take a look at some of them.

Keeping Your Brain Healthy

Taking care of your brain is a lifelong endeavor, and there are countless resources available on the subject. We'll touch upon a few important brain-training tips here, but for more information, check out *Keep Sharp* by neurosurgeon and CNN medical correspondent Sanjay Gupta, MD.

- **Mental stimulation.** Reading, solving puzzles, using brain-training apps, or learning something new, like a language, an instrument, or how to dance—all these activities stimulate the formation of new neural connections.
- **Physical exercise.** Any one will do—and you don't need more than about twenty minutes per day. Exercise stimulates blood flow to your brain, which helps you think clearly and stay sharp.
- **Stress reduction.** Listening to music, meditating—anything that lowers the level of stress hormones in your brain helps with brain fitness.
- **Healthy eating.** Make nutritious food choices, stay away from tobacco, and avoid too much alcohol. Eating healthily involves very personal choices, but it's an important element for a sharp brain.[11]

Neurons That Fire Together Wire Together

Every full moon, groups of people all over the world get together to create rhythms using various kinds of percussion instruments. At these full-moon drum circles, the facilitator starts with an easy rhythm. The next person follows with a rhythm that is maybe a little different, but still in line with the original. That person is followed by another, and another, until there is a really amazing cacophony of sounds. It's easy to get carried away into the rhythm of a drum circle. There's a beautiful synchronicity to it.

My experience in a 2020 drum circle in Bangkok illustrates what research has revealed about how our neurons work: A neuron fires, and others follow in that same rhythm, creating connections. The drum circle started with a slow rhythm that one person played on a cowbell. I felt the rhythm and followed along, playing the bongos. Others started feeling the rhythm as well, and soon I was in a trance of a beautiful rhythmic experience.

This is the way neural connections and pathways are formed. When neurons fire together, they wire together.

In order to create stronger connections and longer-lasting pathways, we have to repeat an experience. Say you're learning a language: If you read a new word in that language once, you will probably remember it for a few minutes. But if you read that word repeatedly over a longer period of time, you will remember it longer. The connections needed to hardwire that word in your brain will have been formed.

It's the same principle at play with your thoughts or experiences. Whether these thoughts are positive or negative, the more time you spend thinking them, or the more times you experience certain things, the more they become hardwired into your brain. So whether it's positive thoughts about how good exercise makes you feel or negative thoughts about not measuring up, if you keep thinking them, they will slowly but surely form strong pathways in your brain.

The thoughts that we accept as true become our beliefs—maps that we use to guide us through life. We'll dive much deeper into that subject later on. For now, keep in mind two vital pieces of information about our beliefs:

- Although our beliefs are sometimes very persistent and strong, we do have the ability to change them.
- If we hold on to outdated beliefs, we may inadvertently act in ways that are misaligned with what is actually going on.

Forming Habits

The connections that form in our brain direct how we live our lives. They create our habits.

Our working memory, sometimes called short-term memory, is where information is stored for a limited period of time. This part of the brain has a finite capacity, but a lot of activity is happening there. In an article published in *Psychological Review*,[12] George Miller reports that we can store seven items in our short-term memory, plus or minus two. Moving information from short- to long-term memory—such as learning to play a musical instrument—takes practice, practice, and more practice.

The reason our brains work so hard to form new neural connections and pathways is to take pressure off our working memory. As soon as a pathway is formed, the information can be stored in our long-term memory, freeing up space and energy from our working memory—and working memory uses a lot of energy.

For example, when we're learning to drive, every step is new, from turning on the ignition to merging onto a busy highway. Do you remember what it was like when you were learning to do these things? Wasn't it exhausting? But after a few months of driving, it became automatic. You didn't really have to think anymore. And that's because the neural pathways had been formed. Your knowledge of how to drive a car was now stored in your long-term memory.

Another interesting thing about working memory is that it does something Ardon Shorr in his TEDx Talk calls "chunking."[13] When we look at a word for the first time, especially when we're learning a new language, we just see individual letters. For example, in the word *R-H-Y-T-H-M* we would see six individual letters. After we have learned the word, we start seeing it as one "chunk." And when we read a sentence like "Rhythm is everywhere around us," we see five chunks that we then combine into a sentence. This is why our brain generally has no problem understanding the meaning of a sentence, even *hwen ew ptu teh ettlers in a dffeiretn sqeuecne!*

In music we do the same thing. The first time we listen to a song, we cannot "chunk" it yet. But as soon as we have heard the song more than once, we start recognizing the pattern: verse, verse, chorus, verse,

verse, chorus, bridge, chorus (or some other variation). A lot of popular songs are built up this way. If you listen to classical music, finding this pattern can be more difficult; the "chunks" are not as obvious. As Shorr explains in his TEDx Talk, the more you begin to enjoy complicated music, the more you start to see the characters, the story. That's why it sometimes takes time to really appreciate certain types of music.

What does chunking have to do with finding *your* rhythm? Simply put, chunking can help you form a new, supportive habit. Because when you can pair a new task with something you already do, you have a better chance of remembering to do it. And remembering is sometimes the hardest part!

For example, if you want to start a meditation habit, and you already have a morning routine that involves brushing your teeth, getting dressed, and drinking coffee, chunk a five-minute meditation with the other tasks. This way, you'll have an easier time remembering to do it. We'll discuss this more in Step 4.

Good Vibrations

Sound is vibration. It has a frequency, a certain rhythm. Frequency can be defined as the number of times a certain event, any event, happens during a certain period of time—like going on vacation twice a year, or having a heartbeat of sixty times per minute. Frequency is often measured in hertz (Hz), which is the number of times a certain event happens per second. So when your heart is beating sixty times per minute, your heartbeat has a frequency of 1 Hz.

Everything on earth has a certain frequency. Our hearts have a frequency, and our brains have a frequency. If the rhythms inside us and those we are exposed to are not aligned, we feel anxious. In other words, if the rhythms within our body are not aligned, or are misaligned with our environment, something feels wrong. So an important question becomes, How can we align all these frequencies, all these rhythms? This interesting quote by Rollin McCraty—a scientist and psychophysiologist, and the executive vice president and director of research at HeartMath Institute—shines a light on how important it is to answer this question:

One of the largest causes of stress for humanity is "the disorganization of heart and mind," which causes an imbalance. "[This inequality] eats the life-force and happiness out of humanity!"[14]

In this book, I will help you learn to align your frequencies, your rhythm. The rhythm of your life. My five-step program will show you how to become aware of your current rhythm, identify the rhythm you would like to have in your life, and take the steps needed to get there.

THE FINDING YOUR RHYTHM PROGRAM

Now that I've explained why finding your rhythm is so important, I'm excited to introduce you to the approach I use to help my clients discover their rhythm. I developed this program over fifteen years, fine-tuning it while working with clients in more than fifty countries.

Each step builds upon the one before it, culminating in you making real changes to move your life in the direction you've envisioned. So let's get started!

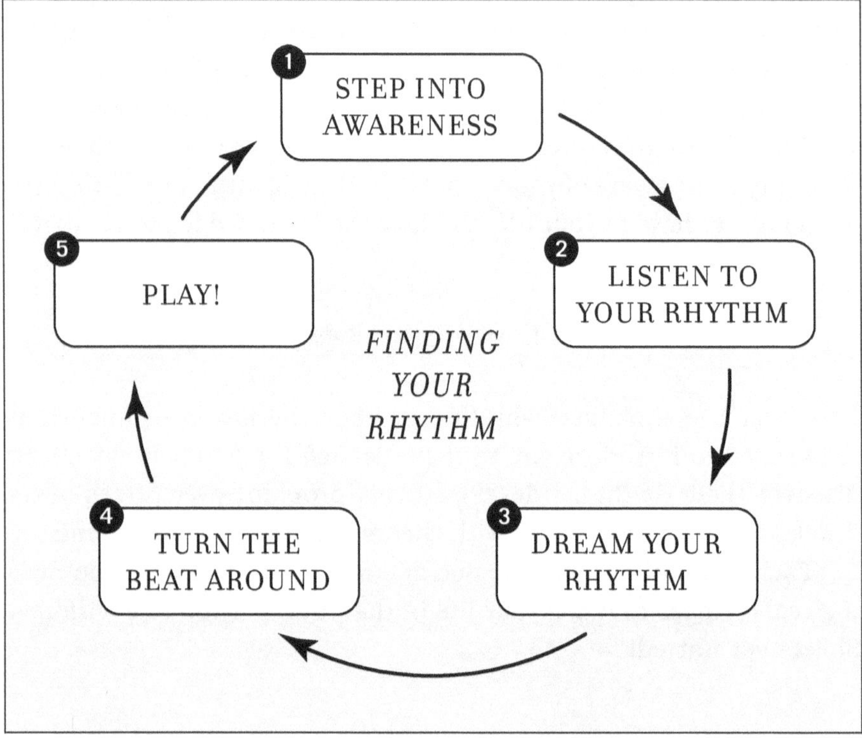

Figure 1. The Finding Your Rhythm program

Step 1: Step into Awareness

In this step you will develop your observation and listening skills to better notice what is going on around and within you. In our busy lives, we have the tendency to keep speeding forward without noticing that life is passing us by. A lot of my clients who are in this state and starting the process of finding their rhythm know that something is wrong. They feel stuck, but they don't know where to begin the process of change. You, too, may be so caught up in the stress of day-to-day life that you can't connect with what's really going on. This is why we start with creating awareness and learning to observe. Without first becoming fully aware, we can't really listen to our rhythm. Step 1 will give you the tools and skills to see your current situation and acknowledge what's working and what isn't.

Step 2: Listen to Your Rhythm

Once you've become more aware, you'll start to hear the rhythm of your current life. Is it fast or slow? Does it have silences? How predictable is your rhythm—does it have a lot of unexpected changes? How connected is it to what's going on around you? Is your rhythm in sync internally?

This step will answer these questions and more. My clients often have many "aha" moments during Step 2. They begin to identify the noise: the things that are holding them back, making them unhappy, or keeping them unfulfilled. And they also start exploring their values and beliefs. When you evaluate the eight dimensions of wellness in this chapter, you will finally start to understand why you are feeling stuck.

Step 3: Dream Your Rhythm

Visioning is an important tool that enables you to set meaningful goals. When you vision the rhythm you would like to create for yourself, you can start hearing it, feeling it, and making it part of who you are. When you clearly hear the rhythm that makes you happy, that's the first step toward creating your perfect life. In Step 3, you'll assess what you're good at, what your goals are, and what your purpose here on earth might be. You'll also learn several techniques for mapping out your future, including the practice of visualization and creating a vision board.

Step 4: Turn the Beat Around

This step is all about moving toward your true rhythm. It's not easy to make changes—if it were, we wouldn't need this book!—but it's easier than you think when you can identify what's blocking you.

Many things can block you from making changes, such as old beliefs. In this step you will learn to get rid of the roadblocks that your mind is putting up. You'll also gear up for new habit formation by developing a clear change plan.

Step 5: Play!

In this step we will explore tools to help you live authentically, based on your true rhythm, and avoid falling back on unwanted rhythms when the going gets tough. This is where all your hard work comes together and you make the changes stick. You are now starting to be the conductor of your own life!

It's time to stop feeling stuck and start discovering your groove. Whether your job or your relationship is making you unhappy, if you're not sure who you are anymore or you're feeling bleak about your future, the Finding Your Rhythm program will put you on track. You will learn about yourself, identify what motivates you, and start making choices that are in harmony with your values. You may be in a rut now, but when you find your rhythm, I promise you'll have a happier, more fulfilling life.

STEP INTO AWARENESS

The less awareness you have, the more you look like others! Increase your awareness, then you will become more unique!

—Mehmet Murat ildan

BEING AWARE

A monk is walking slowly along a road when he hears a galloping sound. He turns around to see a man on horseback moving in his direction. When the man comes closer, the monk asks, "Where are you going?" The man replies, "I don't know. Ask the horse," and rides away.

The horse in this story represents our subconscious mind. If we are not *aware* of our subconscious, it will take us wherever it wants. It will be in charge. And the chatter in our subconscious mind is not always positive or helpful. Researchers found that on a typical day, we have approximately sixty-two hundred thoughts,[15] and our mind has a bias toward negative news.[16] For example, imagine you shared a post on social media and received many positive comments. But there was also one negative comment, saying that your post is ridiculous and stupid. Our subconscious brain has a bias toward this kind of comment; if we aren't aware of that tendency and don't guard against it, we will focus on the negative.[17]

Having awareness means being conscious of what's happening in your environment. It's often sparked by curiosity about what's happening around you. You see how people act and react. You notice how they dress, how they speak, how they move, and how they generally live their lives. But not all of us are aware. Being unaware doesn't mean that you're not curious. It means that you're preoccupied with your own thoughts, your own self.

Being self-aware adds another layer to our consciousness. Though we're not born with this skill, we start developing self-awareness in the first years of life. In research done by Lewis and Brooks-Gunn,[18] a red mark was placed on toddlers' noses, and they were then asked to look in the mirror. Of the children ages fifteen to eighteen months, about 75 percent reached out to touch the red mark in their reflection; only 25 percent reached for their own nose. When the researchers did the same test with children aged twenty-one to twenty-four months, the percentage of children reaching for their own nose jumped to 70 percent.

If you are self-aware, you can recognize what's going on inside of you; this is sometimes called private self-awareness. An example of self-awareness is when you fall in love and notice the butterflies in your stomach every time you see the object of your affection. Or when you're delivering a speech and notice your anxiety and increased heart rate. When you are self-aware, you understand your purpose in your immediate environment. You know your strengths and weaknesses. You know how you relate to the people around you. Armed with this information, you are ready to act in your best interest. If you are aware but not self-aware, you can sometimes feel frustrated by the fact that you understand what's going on but you don't know what to do. It's a bit like the guy on the horse: you know you're sitting on a horse, you see your environment, but you have no idea where the horse is taking you.

Without self-awareness, we might create a rhythm for ourselves that hinders us rather than helping. At one point in my career, I was asked to be managing partner of one of our firm's offices. The office was not performing well. The financial results were bad, the partners were constantly fighting with each other, and employee engagement was very low. I accepted the role and managed to turn the office around, but it had a significant negative impact on my health and personal life.

If I had been more self-aware when I was asked to take on that role, I probably would have said no. But instead I let others determine my rhythm.

So how do we become aware of what's going on in our subconscious mind, and how do we deal with what's happening there? This chapter will answer these questions and get you into awareness mode.

BEING UNAWARE

Let me give you an example of how someone can be completely unaware. It happened to me just now while I was writing: I was typing away on my keyboard when my iPhone pinged. This was a welcome distraction, since I was a bit stuck on how to proceed. When I picked up my phone, I saw that a friend had posted on Instagram. His posts are normally pretty funny, so I opened the app and enjoyed a bit of a laugh. Below my friend's post was a link to a MasterClass course about playing guitar riffs. I am a fanatic guitar player, so I clicked on the link and before I knew it was browsing through the index of all the great courses available on MasterClass. I noticed a photography course by Annie Leibovitz, which reminded me that I had to charge my camera's battery—so I walked to the other room to do that.

Being unaware that I was responding to all the different thoughts popping into my head made me completely lose my focus. Makes you think about the guy on the horse, doesn't it?

We are constantly distracted. Human beings are the only species that has evolved to have the capacity to think about events that aren't happening in the current moment. We can think about things that happened in the past and fantasize about what might happen in the future. This mind wandering is our brain's default status. How many times have you driven somewhere, and when you arrived you thought, *How did I get here?* We can get so lost in our own thinking that we are completely disconnected from what's going on around us.

In 2010, two Harvard psychologists conducted a "happiness study" of 2,250 adults and found that as soon as we disconnect from the present, from what we are experiencing this very moment, our happiness decreases. Their conclusion was that "the human mind is a wandering mind, and a wandering mind is an unhappy mind." This fact that humans can dwell on things that are not occurring, ". . . is a cognitive achievement that comes at an emotional cost."[19]

So why do we keep thinking outside the here and now? Distraction serves a purpose: it allows us to avoid someone or something. When we're distracted, we get temporary relief from whatever we're supposed to be attending to. Let's look at how this played out for one of my clients, a senior sales executive. During one of our sessions, he wondered whether his impulse to browse social media was much stronger when he was having trouble meeting his sales targets. He decided to check out the screen time statistics on his iPhone, and sure enough, he discovered that he was wasting (his own word) a lot more time browsing social media sites during challenging times. Going deeper, he realized that he was distracting himself from the fear of not being successful! So while his job needed his full attention, he unconsciously focused on something that was thwarting his ability to meet his targets. The sales targets grew more daunting every day, and his fear was growing too.

Where do these distractions come from? Since we know that the majority of our thoughts are negative, a good place to look for the source of our distraction is in our own mind. For example, consider how one negative thought can trigger a storm of others:

- *With the company buyout looming, how long will I be able to keep my job?*
- *Will my company start reducing salaries soon?*
- *If I am fired, how will that affect my retirement?*
- *Will my wife stay with me if I lose my job?*
- *That's a strange thought. Does that mean she only loves me for my money?*
- *And what will happen to my children if I can't support them?*
- *Will I ever be able to find another job?*

I can already feel the anxiety in my body, just writing this list of questions. So what do we do to confront these concerns? Most of us let these thoughts give rise to uncomfortable feelings, such as anxiety, sadness, or loneliness, and then, without realizing it, we look for distraction to escape those feelings. Playing video games for hours and hours, binge-watching our favorite Netflix series, drinking alcohol, having sex—there are endless ways we try to run away from being aware and really feeling what we are feeling.

But these thoughts and feelings, and the behaviors resulting from them, will not go away by themselves. Left unattended, the thoughts and feelings may lead to behavior that will probably not create the results you are looking for.

Let's say you are madly in love with a person you recently met at a public speaking workshop. He or she is constantly on your mind, and vice versa. You might have some fears from previous relationships that make you feel scared to open up to this person. *What if I get hurt again? What if they're just interested in me because I have money?* Distracting yourself from these thoughts and feelings will not make them go away. No matter how many Netflix series you watch, and no matter how much sex you have, until you address these thoughts and feelings, they will continue to impact your behavior. And when you are feeling scared, opening up and being able to give and receive real love is going to be difficult, even though real love is what you crave.

So in order to find your rhythm, the first step you need to take is to become aware: of your thoughts, your beliefs, the real reasons behind your actions, and the choices that have led to the life you are living today. Let's explore how to do this.

OBSERVING THE OBSERVER

To understand a little bit more about distractions, awareness, and how the mind works, I'd like you to do one very simple exercise, right now. It will take less time than reading this page. Please try to do the following:

1. Sit down.
2. Close your eyes.
3. Try not to think for one minute.

How was that for you? Were you able to completely eliminate all your thoughts? If you are human and alive, probably not. Our thoughts are there, whatever we do. That is our **thinking mind**, and it goes on and on. This is not inherently bad, of course. We need our thoughts to function and make decisions.

The problems arise when we attach emotions to our thoughts. We can get sucked into our thoughts so deeply that they become our beliefs.

But there is another side to this internal process. When you were doing the exercise, there was also a part of your mind that was "observing" your thoughts. This is your **observing mind**. Your observing mind can notice that your thoughts are just internal creations that are neither good nor bad—nor scared, joyful, worried, excited, or any other emotion. They are just thoughts.

When we don't experience these two parts of the mind—the thinking mind and the observing mind—as separate, we can't separate ourselves from our thoughts and then automatically attach emotions to them.

When you are self-aware, you realize that you are not your thoughts. The thoughts are there, but you can just observe them. When you're more aware of the thinking mind versus the observing mind, you will be able to observe and accept your thoughts and decide whether or not you would like to attach any emotion to them.

The acceptance part of this process is important, and here's why: if you observe the thought and try to resist instead of accepting it, it will only grow stronger. For example, if you have a thought about being nervous when you have to do public speaking, and you actively try to push that thought away, it will only make you more nervous the next time you speak in public. This is because you have attached an emotion to the thought—you've become nervous about being nervous! Now, every time you have a thought about being nervous, you will act nervous.

Instead, when you are faced with an intrusive thought, try to be aware of it and accept that it is there, but don't attach any emotion to it. That will make a big difference in how you respond to it. You can say to yourself, *I'm having the thought that I'm going to be nervous when I do my presentation. That's a valid thought—but not a thought that will help me do my presentation. I'm not actually nervous right now.*

Separating the thinking mind from the observing mind is not an easy process, but it is an important move toward becoming more self-aware. Later in this book we will discuss various meditation techniques that can help you achieve this.

The great thing about self-awareness is that it can put you into action mode. When your thinking mind says, *I'm so angry at my boss,* you can access your observing mind to decide what you would like to do with that thought. Maybe you need to have a meeting with your boss to discuss why you're feeling angry. Or perhaps you need to explore within yourself to understand the cause of your emotion. But you don't need to embody the anger. There is a big difference between thinking, *I'm so angry with my boss,* and, *I feel anger toward my boss.* The former observation will make you stressed, anxious, and probably angrier every minute. With the latter observation, you can start exploring. This process will lead you to being in control of the actions you take.

When we are self-aware, we are open to exploring more of ourselves. We do this by asking ourselves where a feeling is coming from after we have a thought. *Is the feeling coming from a past experience? Am I feeling this way because I don't feel recognized?* There could be many layers to the feeling that you are experiencing. Sometimes it is difficult to get through these layers yourself. Many people work with coaches or therapists who can help "peel the onion."

Once you peel back the layers, you may discover that there is more behind your feelings than you expected—sometimes a lot more. When Maria came to see me, she was feeling sad. She said it was because she'd just broken up with her partner. But when we started to peel the onion, she confessed that breaking up with someone was always considered a very bad thing in her family. Maria believed that her mother wouldn't love her anymore because she'd given up on the relationship too quickly. And Maria needed that love and recognition from her mother. And . . .

Maria's story kept going, and yours might too.

A word of caution: peel the onion carefully. Sometimes people peel back the layers only to find they're getting more and more depressed—and starting to dislike themselves along the way. That is not where you want to go with self-awareness! Start by accepting yourself as you are. Everyone has flaws, including you. True, you're not proud of the terrible things you said to your coworker when your bonus was on the line and he didn't finish the project on time. But you can't change what happened then; you can only change how you'll respond to similar challenges in the future.

When you become self-aware, you can see clearly what you like about yourself and what you don't. Learning how to deal with the things you don't like about yourself, without judgment, is hard work. But I assure you, when you do have the courage to go through this process, it will have a tremendously positive impact on your life. It will decrease or eliminate your negative self-talk, along with the negative things you might think about others.

Keep in mind that this book is not meant for readers experiencing sustained symptoms of depression and is not intended to treat psychological illnesses or disorders. Clinical depression is a serious matter far beyond the scope of this book. If you are experiencing sustained symptoms of depression, I advise you to seek the help of a professional provider.

CREATING AWARENESS

There are many tools and techniques for becoming more aware. Some are easy to use, and others take a bit of practice. Let me name just a few:

- **Meditation**—Meditation can help you observe your thoughts and calm your mind. When you start meditating, you will notice all the thoughts vying for attention in your head, and you can create some distance from them so you don't form emotional attachments.
- **Yoga**—Yoga is a group of physical, spiritual, and mental practices that has been around for a long time. In the past, yoga was practiced to achieve enlightenment. Nowadays, it is used more as exercise connecting body, breath, and mind.

- **Journaling**—The practice of journaling is about exploring your thoughts, feelings, impulses, memories, goals, and hidden desires. It is all about using writing to explore yourself and the life you are living.
- **Listening to and playing music**—Music is important for creating a sense of belonging and community. We are social creatures, and music brings us together: we play music together and we share music, and through these actions we become more aware of each other and our authentic selves.
- **Connecting with nature**—Walking in nature helps us understand that we are part of it. We are part of the constant rhythm that it provides, and we have been for as long as humans have existed. Being away from modern-day distractions enables self-reflection.
- **Travel**—No matter where we go or how far we travel, leaving our day-to-day environment makes us more aware of what's going on around us.

There are many other activities that can help you build awareness and create a more peaceful mind. Some people love to work in the garden. Or ride a motorcycle. Or cook a wonderful meal. The important thing is to challenge yourself to try something new until you discover an activity that helps you learn more about yourself and your surroundings. I hope you'll give at least one of the following activities a try.

Meditation

Vipassana means "to see things as they really are" and is one of India's oldest meditation techniques. Vipassana meditation is a form of meditation that focuses on a deep connection between your body and your mind. The connection is experienced through an intense mindfulness of the physical feelings in your body and then by noticing how these physical feelings feed and connect with your mind.

By focusing on this connection you will be able to understand how your mind and thoughts work and fill your mind with kindness and love through a heightened level of self-awareness.

On the first day of a ten-day Vipassana meditation session I attended, all the participants had to store their books, notepads, phones, computers, smart watches, and any other distractions. It would be ten days without any form of communication. No talking, no gesturing, no eye contact. It was a silent retreat. It would be just me and my thoughts. There was nothing else.

We walked into the center of the room, with men and women on different sides. We were allowed to talk until 8:00 p.m., when the "noble silence" kicked in. People chatted and compared notes on how many times they had experienced a Vipassana meditation.

"I've done it three times now."

"It's great, but not easy!"

"You'll be alone with yourself for ten days, and that can be pretty scary!"

I was getting a bit anxious after hearing remarks like these, and I wasn't particularly looking forward to being with my own thoughts for ten days! There was a pretty strict routine (rhythm) to each day: wake up at 4:00 a.m., meditate, have first meal, meditate, have second meal, attend a lecture, lights out at 9:00 p.m.

The first couple of days were tough. My monkey mind just kept on going. *What the f*?! am I doing here? There is no way I am doing this for ten days! This is really boring, I could have been riding my motorcycle through California!* And so on. There did not seem to be an end to my thoughts.

When we compared notes after the tenth day, we all shared the same experience: "I cannot believe how busy and unstructured my mind was when I started and how focused and sharp my brain became by the tenth day!"

QUIETING THE MONKEY MIND

According to Buddhist principles, the **monkey mind** is unsettled, restless, and confused. It is also closely connected to your ego and wants to be heard all the time. If you are not aware of your monkey mind, it will continuously, subconsciously influence everything you do. It will keep you from finding your rhythm. It will come up with excuses for why things are not possible and reasons why you should just maintain the status quo. The monkey mind presents itself as your biggest supporter, but it's actually your biggest (inner) critic.

You know it's your monkey mind talking when you hear any of the following thoughts:

- a seemingly endless laundry list of to-dos
- fears, whether real or imagined
- hurtful things that happened to you in the past
- judgments about what is happening to you today
- catastrophic what-if scenarios of the future

Have you figured out how "monkey mind" got its name? It resembles a monkey swinging from branch to branch: *I need to put the garbage outside—but I have so much to do for tomorrow—I'm not ready for the presentation I need to give tomorrow—what if it doesn't go well?—I'll probably lose my job—and if I lose my job, how will I be able to take care of my family?—or ever retire?—I'll probably be homeless when I retire . . .* You see where this is going? Nowhere.

But the monkey mind is part of us and always will be. And it can actually be helpful, because it reminds us of things we need to do. The trick is to train your monkey mind not to jump from branch to branch so often. So how can you do that? It starts with being aware of your monkey mind. When you notice your thoughts swinging wildly, it might be time for a meditation break; you'll get tips for meditating in the coming pages.

It's also important to watch what you eat and drink. There are certain things we consume—sugar, chocolate, gluten, alcohol, caffeine, and energy drinks, for example—that cause neurochemical reactions in our brain, activating the monkey mind and making it very hard to stay in the present.

FROM THE BODHI TREE TO BUDDHIFY

Meditation has really gained popularity over the last few decades. Apps like Headspace and Buddhify are used by millions of people around the world. Also, it's becoming harder and harder to sign up for ten-day Vipassana courses—most centers now have waiting lists for every retreat!

So where did all this sudden interest in meditation come from?

Meditation has been around for a long time. We don't know exactly how long, since in the early days, gurus taught their students through discussions and lecturing. The first documented evidence of people sitting in meditation poses dates back to between 5000 and 3500 BC. Evidence of written forms of meditation dates back to 1500 BC.

Historical evidence also shows that meditation has long been linked to spiritual practices. When people think about meditation, they often think of Buddhism, which was founded by Siddhārtha Gautama in approximately 500 BC. Siddhārtha, who would later become the "Buddha," was raised as a prince. There are many sources describing the life of Siddhārtha. The *Buddhacarita* is the first full biography, written by the poet Aśvaghoṣa in the first century AD. As the story goes, Siddhārtha's parents protected him from all suffering, and his early years were very lavish, but as he grew older, he became more curious about what was going on outside the palace. One day he escaped the palace and witnessed suffering for the first time. He saw people who were sick and even dying—sights he'd been protected from when he was living inside the palace walls. Moved by the suffering in the world, he decided to exchange his princely lifestyle for one of poverty and denial. He left the palace and began his spiritual journey.

When he realized that poverty also did not fulfill him, he started promoting the idea of the "middle way"—a life without extremes, without the social indulgences but also without deprivation. If you are interested in reading more about the story of Siddhārtha, I highly recommend the book *Siddhartha* by Hermann Hesse.[20]

It is believed that the Buddha achieved a state of enlightenment later in his life, while sitting under a bodhi tree. He spent the rest of his days teaching others about his spiritual path.

Meditation is also practiced as part of other spiritual paths and religions, such as Hinduism, Taoism, and Christianity.

TYPES OF MEDITATION

Using a religious/spiritual framework, some of the more popular meditation styles can be categorized as shown in the table below.[21] This is not meant to be an exhaustive list, but rather as an indication that there are many different forms of meditation.

Buddhist	*Hindu*
Vipassana meditation	*yoga meditation*
zazen meditation	*mantra meditation*
mindfulness meditation	*Transcendental Meditation*
metta meditation	*I Am meditation*
Taoist	*Christian*
Taoist meditation	*contemplative prayer*
qigong meditation	*contemplative reading*

Figure 2. Types of meditation

I AM NOT GOING TO SIT ON A PILLOW AND BREATHE!

Peter walked into my office. A few weeks before, we'd spoken on the phone and he'd told me he was stuck. He was not happy with his life but did not know where to start to make a change. When clients go through big changes in their lives, I usually invite them to spend a week in my guesthouse in Bali to have time for themselves outside their normal environment; during this time, the client has daily coaching sessions with me and completes exercises. Peter knew he needed to make a big shift, so he took me up on my invitation.

He arrived late in the afternoon, and after spending some time sitting and looking at the sea, we had dinner. I noticed that Peter was tense. He was moving his body all the time and had a big frown line between his eyebrows; even the way he moved revealed that he was in a constant state of hypertension. I felt sympathy for him. As a coach, I like to see my clients happy, and Peter definitely was not. After dinner I went through the program with him. I informed him that his first task was to get up at 6:00 a.m. and meditate.

Peter: What?! Meditate? But Karel, you know I'm a partner in the largest global consulting firm, don't you? I came here to be coached by you. I was hoping you could help me get my energy back. You are a leadership coach, aren't you?
Me: Have you done any meditation before?
Peter: No. Meditation is what monks do. They sit on a pillow and chant the whole day. I have more important things to do!
Me: Can you tell me about these "more important things," and how doing these things makes you feel?
Peter: Just important things. Big client projects. Managing people. Solving all kinds of important issues. And how do they make me feel? Well, uhm, I guess they make me feel important. They make me feel I achieved something in my life. But . . . I guess doing all these important things also brought me to where I am today. And the reason I'm here is that I don't feel very happy with what I'm doing.
Me: Peter, what if I told you that it has been scientifically proven that people who meditate have lower blood pressure, are able to deal with stress a lot better, are much more focused, are calmer, and as a result have more clarity on where they would like their lives to go. Would you be willing to give it a try?

Needless to say, Peter did show up at 6:00 a.m. for a meditation session. He reminded me years later that this first session was when he started discovering a spiritual part of himself that he had never explored before. He even sat for a ten-day Vipassana retreat ten years after that first introduction to meditation!

HOW TO START A MEDITATION PRACTICE

Starting a meditation practice is daunting to a lot of people. So let me put some fears to rest: I will not ask you to just sit on a meditation cushion, burn some incense, and try to think about nothing.

In fact, meditation is easier than you think. It basically involves setting your mind to do it and then making it a regular practice. There are hundreds of resources to help you get started: books, online training courses, meditation groups, and of course a number of really good meditation apps. Apps such as Chopra, Buddhify and Headspace offer great guided meditations. Muse (ChooseMuse.com) is another beginner's app. It comes with a Muse Headband that tracks your meditation progress by measuring your brainwave activity and giving you a very good sense of how you were able to enter into and stay in your relaxed state. The newest version also measures heartbeat and breathing—what else do you need to ensure that your body rhythm is completely in sync?

I recommend starting with a meditation session every morning to set the tone for the rest of your day. But there are also people who prefer to meditate before bedtime, after their minds have been racing all day. It's a good practice to get prepared for sleep.

Yoga

Yoga might seem like an invention of twentieth-century fitness clubs, but it dates back a bit further than that. The first known references to yoga practice are from five thousand years ago. The early yogic writings were done on palm leaves and consisted of sacred texts that had previously been transmitted orally. As you can imagine, after five thousand years those palm leaves are pretty hard to read!

The history of yoga is typically broken into five stages:

- **Vedic period (ca. 4000–2500 BC)**—The word *yoga* was first mentioned in the Rig Veda. The Vedas contained mantras and rituals used by the Vedic priests, the Brahmans, who mainly lived in India. The Vedas were characterized by ceremonies and rituals that encouraged broadening the mind to surpass its limitations.

- **Preclassical period (ca. 2500–200 BC)**—In this period, the Upanishads—a collection of two hundred Vedic texts—were created. When you start exploring yoga, you will probably run into the Bhagavad Gita, which was written in Sanskrit and is one of the most renowned yogic scriptures, presented as a narrative between Pandava prince Arjuna and his guide and charioteer, Krishna, an avatar of Lord Vishnu. It is generally considered a comprehensive and easy-to-understand summary of Vedic knowledge—in other words, the most important lessons from the Upanishads.
- **Classical period (ca. 200 BC–AD 500)**—Patanjali, a sage living in India, is said to be the author of the Yoga Sutras, a classical yoga text. In the 196 Sanskrit sutras that are part of the text, Patanjali organized and synthesized the knowledge from many older yogic traditions. The Yoga Sutras still have a strong influence on modern yoga.
- **Postclassical period (ca. AD 500–AD 1900)**—After the classical yoga period, many satellite traditions of yoga started to form. Examples are the Bhakti movement, Hindu Tantra, Tantric Buddhism, Zen Buddhism, Sikhism, and Hatha Yoga. Hatha Yoga combines elements of the Yoga Sutras with postures (asanas) and breathing exercises. It's the style most associated with yoga studios today.
- **Modern period (ca. AD 1900–present)**—In the nineteenth and twentieth centuries, there were many yoga masters who traveled to the West to lecture. Since then, yoga has attracted many followers, and yoga training centers have been established all around the world.

WHY YOGA?

The purpose of yoga is to build strength, awareness, and harmony in both the mind and the body. When people think about yoga, they mostly think of the incredibly difficult (for most of us) postures. But there is so much more to the practice. According to Ananda Balayogi Bhavanani, yoga is a way of living where "awareness and consciousness play a great part in guiding our spiritual evolution through life."[22]

Practicing yoga has many health benefits. For a start, the relaxation techniques can ease chronic pain, lower blood pressure, and reduce insomnia. YogaJournal.com lists thirty-five additional physical, mental, and spiritual benefits, including increased flexibility, muscle strength and tone, happiness, and self-esteem, as well as healthier, stronger, and happier relationships, just to name a few.

With all these benefits, it makes you wonder why everyone isn't hooked on yoga!

IS YOGA FOR EVERYONE?

Broadly speaking, yes—yoga is something that virtually everyone of any ability and nearly any age can do. So why don't more people practice yoga? The main arguments seem to be not having the time for it or being too stiff to do it.

Let's talk first about being too stiff. I have been extremely tight and stiff all my life. I never stretched before exercising, and I've worked in an office most of my career. My fitness level was OK thanks to regular running, but I sensed that my flexibility and strength were declining as I aged.

After reading the book *Younger Next Year: Live Strong, Fit, Sexy, and Smart—Until You're 80 and Beyond*,[23] I started thinking about what kind of exercise I could switch to. I had been a runner for years and had finished a half marathon in an hour and fifty-five minutes, which I thought was a pretty good time for my age. But I felt I needed to build some strength and flexibility.

"How do you think you'll ever be able to do yoga?" was my friends' reaction when I suggested I might try it. "You can't even touch your knees!"

As you can imagine, I was a bit reluctant to start. Like many people are.

But one weekend I woke up and thought, *This is my day.* I picked up my exercise clothes and headed to the gym, where I was a member.

I got on the BTS (the skytrain in Bangkok, where I lived at that time) and was excited when I arrived at the gym.

"*Sawasdee ka*, Mr. Bakkes," said the woman behind the reception desk.

I smiled, waved, and made my way to the changing room. After putting on my workout clothes, I walked over to the yoga room. Everyone was dressed in expensive Lululemon gear; they looked lean and polished and very experienced and serious, as if they belonged in a fitness magazine. I made my way to an empty yoga mat and the class started. And what a start! Within minutes, the whole class was tied up in positions that I didn't even know were humanly possible. A bit disheartened, I left the class and headed for the treadmill.

Luckily, a few weeks later, I ran into someone who owned a yoga studio in Bangkok. I told her my story and she had to laugh.

"Yes, in most gyms that's the way it is. Most people go to the gym to exercise, and that's how they practice yoga in the gym—pushing themselves like they're in a competition. For yoga, it doesn't really matter whether your fingers can reach your thighs, your knees, or the ground when you bend forward. There are actually modifications for every yoga pose and beginner classes in every style."

Her encouraging words enticed me to give it another try, and I've been hooked ever since. Practicing yoga regularly has significantly increased my strength and flexibility. Now trust me, I will never be able to bend in the ways that a lot of yogis can, but that's not the point. The idea is to explore your limits, to get in tune with your body and your inner self.

This book is all about making that happen for you—taking the steps to change your rhythm. And starting with yoga could be one of those first moves. If you need more motivation, keep in mind that yoga can be a very good way to increase your awareness—of your body and mind, along with your sensations, emotions, and breathing. You will need this awareness to take stock of where you are in your life when we proceed to Step 2 of the Finding Your Rhythm program.

HOW TO START A YOGA PRACTICE

There are many ways to start a yoga practice. The easiest options are to watch yoga lessons on YouTube or subscribe to a yoga app, such as Glo. But to ensure you get the proper guidance, find a yoga studio—one that practices and teaches yoga as a way of life, not just as exercise. This means that the studio may also offer guided meditations or workshops in breath work, lowering stress, or even healthy eating.

Please don't get sidetracked by the incredibly complicated poses you see online and on social media. No matter your body type or flexibility level, there is a yoga style for everyone.

Finally, don't get discouraged if the first class or studio you try isn't a good fit. When I was living in Beijing, I had a negative experience with a yoga teacher. He was from India and had been doing yoga since he was three years old. He was convinced that if he just pushed and pulled people into poses, our bodies would surrender and become flexible. Unfortunately, that did not work for me (and many others), and I ended up with a back injury that required months of recuperation.

So if a teacher doesn't feel right for you, don't wait to find another one. Follow your gut. Studios have different agendas, as do the instructors who work there. You may need to try out a number of different classes or teachers before finding the best match—a lot like dating! It's just part of the process.

You'll know you've found the right studio or teacher when you are physically and mentally challenged to the point where you are improving and motivated to keep your practice going. Here are some practical tips for finding the right yoga teacher and studio:

- **Define your goal.** Find a yoga style that matches your objective for learning yoga. Would you like more of a spiritual emphasis, or do you want to get into better physical shape, or both? If you are just starting, are not a very physical person, or would like to focus more on the spiritual side of the practice, Ananda, Yin, or Restorative Yoga might be good options for you. If you're more physically inclined, Vinyasa and Ashtanga Yoga are good choices.

- **Find an expert.** Look at the teachers' experience. Many people have completed 200-hour yoga teacher training these days, but some might not have much teaching experience yet. Ensure that the teaching team includes some experienced teachers.
- **Check accreditation.** Many schools are Yoga Alliance accredited. Although some excellent schools might not be accredited, the accreditation gives you a first indication of the quality of the lessons being offered.

Once you start practicing yoga, you will see results pretty quickly. Typically, yoga teachers advise their students to do yoga three to five times per week, allowing time to rest in between. The frequency does depend heavily on your own ambition and body type. If you make it a habit to practice three to five times per week, you will see and feel changes in your physical body quickly—as early as four to six weeks.

It will likely take more time to see results in your spiritual health, but the rate of improvement is very different for every individual.

Another way to get a head start on making yoga part of your life is to attend a yoga retreat. Such retreats are offered all over the world. From personal experience, I know there are really good ones in Bali. It makes for a great excuse to take a vacation—you deserve it! Plus it can be easier to start building a yoga habit during a five-to-ten-day yoga retreat, with full focus and guidance, than to try working it into your day-to-day life.

As with starting any new practice, getting to a basic level of proficiency physically or spiritually is not that difficult. Staying with it to get good or become an expert takes a lot of time and hard work. But even moderate effort will reap important health benefits.

And before I forget: if you do decide to take yoga lessons at the gym, make sure you stop by Lululemon first!

Journaling

"Journaling? Really? I thought only teenage girls kept journals. How in the world would journaling be of any benefit to me? I am an executive.

I pay you to coach me. And after listening to my problems, all you can suggest is that I start journaling?"

It was clear that Bridget, the CEO of a global food company, was not enthusiastic about starting a daily journal. And yet journaling is one of the most effective ways to sort out problems and discover authentic, workable solutions. In Bridget's case, her "problem" was her tendency to get stuck in the same negative thought pattern. Unfortunately, she wasn't even aware of her thinking habits.

Moreover, the emotions that she attached to her thoughts were intense, preventing her from thinking clearly. Bridget was stuck in her own head. I knew journaling would help her become unstuck, but she needed some convincing to adopt this daily practice.

WHY YOU CAN'T SEEM TO THINK CLEARLY

The **amygdala** is the place in the brain where we process strong feelings, like pleasure and fear. Part of the brain's limbic system, it is constantly reviewing the sensory signals that come through. Its main function is processing fear stimuli. When information about a fearful stimulus is received, the amygdala sends signals to other parts of the brain to activate, for example, a fight-or-flight reaction. Some fear stimuli reach our amygdala even before we are consciously aware of the potential danger. In addition to processing fear stimuli, the amygdala also helps store and form memories of past events that made us fearful. In a study using rhesus monkeys in the 1930s,[24] researchers found that removing the amygdala from the monkeys' brain made them much more relaxed; they did not show many signs of fear.

In prehistoric times, the amygdala was put to really good use. It was constantly scanning the environment, and if it detected danger, it would jump into action, bypassing the more conscious or thinking part of the brain and sending quick signals to other parts to initiate a fight-or-flight reaction. This is helpful, because if there's a big animal wanting to eat you for lunch, you don't need your brain to first consider what type of animal it is or any other unessential analytical questions. No, you need to run.

So what happens to your body when the amygdala sends the danger signal? Your heart starts beating faster, stress hormones are released, your blood pressure rises. All these happen as a result of the amygdala's outputs. And with real danger, that is a good thing!

Numerous tests have shown how the amygdala helps us learn to recognize dangers. The tests generally involved a sensory signal combined with something painful, such as a loud sound followed by an electric shock. One such experiment was performed by John Watson and Rosalie Rayner with an infant named Albert.[25] To start, Albert was exposed to a white rat. He had no fear reaction to the rat. Subsequently, the researchers loudly hammered on a steel pipe every time Albert saw the rat. Albert began to associate the loud noise with the rat and would cry each time he saw it, assuming the loud noise would follow. The amygdala learned pretty quickly that the sight of the rat meant distress (the loud sound) was coming, so it would put the body in a state of emergency (crying for help).

As we can deduce from the experiment, the problem with the amygdala is that it can sometimes be inappropriately aroused. This is called an **amygdala hijack**. In an inappropriately aroused state, our brain can compel us to react as if we're threatened even if we're not; our amygdala doesn't know the difference between a physical threat and a psychological one. In an aroused state, your amygdala will generalize. It will associate sensory input in a way that does not reflect the real situation.

Let's say you meet a client for the first time and his voice reminds you of the boy who bullied you for years in high school. You feel the instant urge to get away from this person (or maybe you want to fight back), as your body goes into panic mode. In the presence of a real threat, these urges and sensations might keep you safe; in the absence of a real threat, they might wind up losing you a client!

Why am I telling you all this? Because unwarranted, excessive fear and anxiety is a sign of amygdala hijack, which reduces our capacity to process and store information. When you are in this state, you have a really hard time thinking clearly and making the right decisions.

AVOIDING AMYGDALA HIJACK

Let's face it: the ability to regulate our emotions is a very valuable tool that can help us in both our personal and our private lives. Fortunately, researcher have been looking at ways we can regulate our emotions,[26] especially the ones triggered by the fight-or-flight response, and particularly when the threat isn't real. They found that when you create more activity in your brain's problem-solving areas—for example, by talking about or naming your feelings—your amygdala calms down. As a result, your body will be more relaxed, and you will be able to think more clearly and make the right decisions.

And guess what? Journaling is another way to activate the problem-solving part of the brain.

Keeping a journal has been a key habit of many successful people throughout the ages. Benjamin Franklin, Virginia Woolfe, Bob Dylan, and John D. Rockefeller were all said to keep daily journals. Supposedly, the earliest known daily journal was kept by the Roman emperor Marcus Aurelius.

"That all sounds great," said Bridget, "but what do I write about? And how should I start?"

HOW TO START A JOURNALING PRACTICE

There are no specific rules for journaling, but building it into a daily (or even weekly) routine will be the most effective way to get out of your head, unclutter your mind, and invite calm. Some people, including me, write immediately after waking up, to ensure their mind is still completely fresh. I try to journal right after my morning exercise and meditation. Others prefer to write as part of a bedtime routine. When you decide to journal is up to you; just make sure it's at a time when you can write uninterrupted. And make it a habit.

You don't need a lot to get started with journaling. Just buy a blank notebook, open an electronic file, or download a journaling app such as Day One or Reflectly, and begin writing. Set aside fifteen to thirty minutes each day as a starting point, and write down anything that comes to mind—any thought or issue you're struggling with or that needs some attention. Don't give it too much thought. Try to just keep writing.

And remember, your journal doesn't need to become a *New York Times* bestseller. So don't worry about typos, or sentence structure, or what people would think if they read it. This journal is for you and only you.

If you have a hard time starting, it may help to reflect on your values and gratitude list (more on that in the following chapter).

You might also ask yourself,

- *How am I feeling?*
- *What am I grateful for?*
- *What did I do yesterday that gave me a lot of energy?*
- *What did I do yesterday that drained my energy?*
- *Is the way I am living my life still aligned with my values? (More on values in Step 2.)*
- *What were the most positive and negative feelings I experienced yesterday?*
- *How have I been spending my time?*

Make it a weekly or monthly habit to review what you wrote. When you can reflect on your experiences and learnings, you will become more aware of what you truly enjoy doing and what gives you the most energy. While reflecting on your experiences, try to find patterns in the things you did, how you were feeling, what you were thinking. Ask yourself, *What have I learned from reflecting on my experiences? Are there any lessons I've learned that I can start applying in my life going forward?*

During my final coaching session with Bridget, I invited her to share what had been most impactful in getting her unstuck.

"You probably won't believe it," she said, "but the journaling part has been a door opener for me. I was very skeptical in the beginning, but by reading through my journal after I made it a habit to journal every day, I realized important patterns that were significantly holding me back in both my private and professional life."

Listening to and Playing Music

Music moves us. Certain songs or lyrics can bring back memories and invoke different emotions—sadness, happiness, anger, love. We all have our favorite songs that we play when we're in certain moods. Likewise, music can be an excellent mood *changer*. It can also keep us focused on the present moment.

In the Harvard study on the link between wandering minds and unhappiness,[27] the researchers found that certain types of activities make the mind wander more or less. It wanders most when we do things like working, commuting, or browsing the internet; it wanders least while we're making love. And second to making love is playing and listening to music. In other words, when we play or listen to music, our mind is focused on the present moment. Imagine what would happen if you made love and listened to music at the same time!

Remember, a wandering mind is an unhappy mind. When our minds are focused, our chances of feeling happy are much higher. That is obviously a great place to start in terms of developing self-awareness.

Music has the power to tap into the subconscious part of the brain. In an experiment with veterans suffering from post-traumatic stress disorder,[28] researchers wanted to know whether group drumming could decrease PTSD symptoms. One of their findings was that it brought back memories of traumatic events. The rhythmic sounds reminded participants of the shooting or the chaos surrounding them at the time of their trauma. In another experiment, researchers found that listening to specific musical components actually changes how people think.[29] In other words, by connecting us to the subconscious part of our brain, music and rhythm provide an opportunity to increase self-awareness.

Sharing music with others is an activity that a lot of people really enjoy. Since music is so linked to your personal feelings and emotions, you show others a little bit of your true self when you share music that touches you. The process of browsing through your music, thinking about certain songs and the emotions attached to them, is a very reflective exercise. It requires concentration and going inside yourself to learn which songs touch you and tell a story that you would like to convey.

The story of the jazz singer Melody Gardot is a great example of the power of music. Melody was involved in a traffic accident when she was in her late teens; at the time, she had been studying fashion in Philadelphia. As a result of the accident, Melody suffered short-term memory loss and experienced a condition call anomic aphasia, which caused her to struggle to translate her thoughts into speech. Her doctor suggested music therapy, through which she was able to get her speech and short-term memory back. In an interview with the *Irish Times*, Melody explained how music therapy facilitated her recovery. She describes how music "reconnects neural pathways and activates other parts of the mind . . . it activates the brain at a high level." She goes on to explain that the music worked in her brain with her memory as well as her vocal and physical skills. All of this together helped her talk again.[30]

So yes, music moves us. But it can do much more than just that. Music has the power to heal us.

Connecting with Nature

We are all part of nature, but sometimes we forget that. Actually, not sometimes. It seems like humanity has almost completely forgotten about nature. How much time do we spend walking outside, even if it's just in a city park? How often do we take the time to lie on our backs in the grass and look at the stars? With all the busyness around us, we cannot seem to find the time. Yet most of us have experienced, at least once or twice, how being connected to nature increases our awareness and can bring us a true sense of being in the present moment.

By forgetting about nature, we have created a lot of problems—climate change, pollution, and the extinction of many animal species are just some examples. On the other hand, it is scientifically proven that connecting with nature positively impacts our health and happiness. A study by Thompson et al. found a very high correlation between someone's stress levels and the lack of "green" in their environment.[31] Simply putting plants in certain spaces, such as offices or hospitals, had a significant positive impact on the people nearby. The researchers found that being in nature, or being exposed to scenes from nature, reduces anger, fear, and stress and increases positive feelings. And vice versa: an urban environment actually increases stress levels, as a result of all the non-natural stimuli.

Research conducted by Ming Kuo, at the University of Illinois, found that people with some natural elements in their environment functioned better socially, psychologically, and physically than those without. Working with residents of several similar buildings, he put trees and plants around only a few of the buildings. He then measured the crime rates, empathy levels, neighborhood relations, and health status of the people living in the buildings. The conclusion was very clear: the buildings surrounded by trees and plants scored better on all fronts![32]

Let's go back to the topic of awareness. Given the impact that nature has on our stress levels and our ability to relax and connect, taking a trip out in nature—or at least creating an environment for yourself where there are elements of nature—can significantly increase your awareness levels. It also does wonders for your mental health.[33] I always find it amazing how much more focused and productive I am when, instead of diving headfirst into the busy Bangkok public transportation system every morning, I take the time to start my day with a walk or run in the city park.

THE WISDOM IN INDIGENOUS PRACTICES

Indigenous peoples around the globe have a very strong connection to nature, as evidenced by the traditions of the Maori in New Zealand, the Maasai in Kenya and Tanzania, the hill tribes in Thailand, and the Native Americans in the United States, just to name a few.

While much of the modern world seems to view nature as a commodity, with misplaced regard for the delicate ecosystems in our various biospheres, indigenous cultures who live closest to the land and depend on it for survival tend to honor rather than desecrate their surroundings. According to the World Health Organization, there are an estimated 370 million indigenous people formed into five thousand tribes, living in more than seventy countries worldwide. And although indigenous people make up no more than 5 percent of the planet's population, they safeguard about 25 percent of the land. Even more important, they safeguard 80 percent of the global biodiversity![34]

In an article in HuffPost, Nina Wegner, cofounder of the Vanishing Cultures Project, wrote about progress. She explains how our world is currently dedicated to "progress at all costs," which consequently causes a multitude of issues with climate, energy, treatment of land, and many other international concerns. She wonders how much our world's advances help us as she cleverly points out, "Most indigenous cultures . . . were able to live sustainably for centuries."[35]

We can learn a lot from the traditional wisdom of these stewards of the earth, because it's important for all of us to ensure a balance between the resources Mother Earth offers and the resources we consume. When I was living in New Zealand, I had the privilege of being introduced to the Maori culture, whose wisdom and indigenous practices can be seen in everyday Kiwi life.

An important aspect of how Maori look at nature is interconnectedness. As do many indigenous cultures across the globe, Maori people consider nature a fundamental part of human existence. While in most Western thinking, nature belongs to man, Maori look at this relationship another way: man belongs to nature. In the Maori language, the word for indigenous people is *Tangata Whenua*, meaning "the people of the land."

Another Maori word—*kaitiakitanga*—describes their strong sense of respect for and guardianship over the natural environment, born of their beliefs about how the world was created. These beliefs personify the various forces and functions of nature, resulting in a world that can be traced directly back to the divine.

One situation that highlights the interconnectivity of all elements of nature occurred when the British introduced foreign animals to New Zealand in the nineteenth century, throwing the whole ecosystem—with its unique climate, flora and fauna, and divers geography developed over eons, separate from other land masses—out of balance.

Fortunately, the Maori people and the New Zealand government have done a lot to protect their country's wilderness from further damage. For example, after 160 years of fighting legal battles, the Maori succeeded in getting legal protection for the Whanganui River, one of the country's most important natural resources: in 2017, the river became the first in the world to be recognized as a legal person! To ensure that their knowledge of nature is used in present-day legislation and decisions about the environment, the Maori continue to be involved in New Zealand's government.

As a result of all this hard work, New Zealand has been globally regarded as a hotspot for biodiversity since the concept was introduced at the Rio de Janeiro Earth Summit in 1992.

We can learn a lot from the Maori knowledge that has been passed on through many generations. If we could start seeing the world as something that we are all part of, or even something more holy, we would probably have much greater respect for the beautiful planet we live on!

THE POWER OF NATURE

Nature has an uncanny way of slowing us down. Most of us enter wild spaces with a go-go-go attitude and an agenda: climb a certain peak, swim a certain distance, bike across a canyon floor, pitch a tent for a night or two. But when you spend extended time in nature, or you intentionally let go of any plan, something magical happens. Your pace slows, your muscles relax, your manner of speaking may even change. This is you adjusting to the rhythm of nature!

Let's look at how Peter was impacted by nature during his Finding Your Rhythm journey. As you may recall, Peter was not very enthusiastic when I suggested meditation on his first day. But he did end up joining me for meditation, and after we meditated and had breakfast, I informed him that we were going on a two-hour silent walk through nature.

Peter: A what? A silent walk? What does that mean?
Me: It means exactly what it says. We are going to walk in a beautiful area of Bali where we will not see other people, and we'll be silent the whole time we walk.
Peter: Two hours of not speaking? Why? How does that help? I'd like to tell you about the things that are bothering me, and I'd like you to help me with them. That's why I'm here!
Me: I know this is something you aren't used to doing, but please trust me on this one. During our walk I will also put a blindfold on you, and we will walk hand in hand for about thirty minutes.
Peter: Excuse me?! Walk hand in hand? With a blindfold? I will look like a complete idiot!
Me: [*Laughing*] The benefit of walking through nature where there is absolutely no one around is that no one will notice.

At the start of our route, we spoke for a few minutes. Then we agreed to be silent and just experience nature for the next two hours. I led Peter first through an area with a lot of trees, and then to a beach. Then I put the blindfold on him. Initially he resisted, but he began to loosen up after a while. I could even sense him open up while we were walking. In fact, he almost seemed disappointed when I took the blindfold off after thirty minutes! By then Peter's pace had slowed down, and he would stop occasionally to look around. When we finished our walk, we sat down on a rock overlooking the sea. I asked Peter what he had experienced.

Peter: Karel, you have no idea what just happened to me. When we started walking, I was still very busy in my head. Thoughts were going everywhere. *Why am I doing this? Is he really going to blindfold me? What will people say when they see me walking around like this?* But after some time, the thoughts became quieter. I started to hear the songs the birds were singing. I started to hear the leaves moving in the wind. The cracking of twigs underneath my feet. I felt the wind on my face and smelled the salty air as we came closer to the sea. And all of these sensory experiences multiplied when you blindfolded me! It really slowed me down; I think for the first time in a long time I felt "in the moment." I wasn't thinking about all the things I should have done differently or the things that might go wrong in the future. I was just experiencing the *now*! Thank you!

And this is what nature does to us. We are nature. When we become aware, we start feeling our connection to the earth again. We start respecting nature again. We start feeling at home.

HOW TO CONNECT WITH NATURE

From the perspective of physiological anthropology, we human beings have lived in the natural environment for most of the five million years of our existence. Therefore our physiological functions are most suited to natural settings.[36] Many studies have been done supporting the idea that connecting regularly with nature results in better health and improved well-being: lower blood pressure, reduced stress, and better mental health are just a few of the proven benefits. That does not mean that you have to move to a greener environment or to the mountains. But a 2017 study published in *Scientific Reports* does suggest that if you reside in a city, you should consider spending at least 120 minutes per week connecting with nature.[37] Although the researchers included a number of qualifiers about your level of activity and the richness of the biodiversity in your area, the 120 minutes seems like a good starting point. So how to get started?

There are many simple things you can do to hit that starting point. If you live in a city, go to the park. And if you have the time, get out of the city at least once a month to experience real nature. If you struggle to venture out on your own, join a hiking club. If you don't like hiking, simply observe nature. Get your camera out and take some pictures. Or go for a picnic. Just *being* in nature has a tremendous impact.

The Japanese practice of forest bathing, or *shinrin-yoku*, is another way to get started. Shinrin-yoku is a practice that helps you completely relax and take in the forest atmosphere. It is not exercise; it is being in nature—walking slowly, looking around, listening to your footsteps, feeling the wind on your face, touching the trees, putting your hands in running water. If you like, combine it with yoga, tai chi, or meditation. And no, I do not want to see your shinrin-yoku experience on Instagram. Leave your electronics at home and really try to be there.

Believe me, it'll be worth it. A Japanese study found that the benefits of forest bathing included a lower pulse rate, significantly increased vigor, and less depression, fatigue, anxiety, and confusion.[38] What are you waiting for?

Travel

In the epigraph to his 1919 book *The Travel Diary of a Philosopher*, Hermann von Keyserling wrote, "The shortest path to oneself leads around the world."[39]

When we travel, whether it's a short vacation or living for a longer time in a foreign country, we are exposed to new cultures and new ways of doing things. Often these different experiences take us out of our comfort zone—and that's where we learn. Though travel is not the only way for us to become more self-aware, it can definitely help!

When I think about getting out of my comfort zone and traveling, my thoughts always go to my grandparents. My grandfather was a missionary; he and my grandmother moved to Celebes, Indonesia, in 1925. In her memoirs, my grandmother wrote about making the trip to Indonesia: first by train from the Netherlands to Italy, then by boat to Jakarta, then by another boat to Celebes. In Celebes there were no roads to the place they were headed, so they had to travel on horseback. Compare that to the way we travel these days!

My grandparents' journey was obviously a lot more intense than a vacation to another part of the world or a work transfer to another country, but any trip you take to a place different from your usual environment will give you opportunities to self-reflect and learn more about who you really are—not just because of the "me time" you often get when you travel, but also because traveling exposes you to new perspectives from seeing a different way of life, having conversations with strangers who share their stories with you, learning about the prevalent religion in the country you're visiting, or any other experience that's different from what you're used to.

Many years ago, I had dinner with a participant in a workshop I was running with my partner. His name was Taffy. Taffy was blind and originally from Zimbabwe; while we ate, he shared his life story with me. He told me that his parents died from AIDS when he was young. He lived on the streets until he was picked up and brought to an orphanage—but he was beaten and abused while living there. When he was eighteen, he managed to get away and found someone who believed in him and helped him become a strong athlete. His life turned around. After enduring all those hardships, he'd finally found himself in sports. However, when he was twenty-three, he developed a disease that caused him to lose his eyesight.

I asked him if he'd ever considered giving up on life after going through so many terrible experiences. He stopped eating his dinner and said, "Really? Giving up on life? After all the things I learned and the lessons I can now bring to kids in similar situations? I have learned how to crawl up every time life brings me down. It would be such a waste if I did not share these lessons with others!"

The way Taffy shared his experiences was by setting up a foundation in Zimbabwe that focused on bringing sports to people who were visually impaired. After we'd finished our dinner, as Taffy walked away, I saw the slogan on the back of his T-shirt: Life Is Good.

Taffy's message inspired me to take a close look inside myself. I am still grateful every day for having heard that perspective.

KEY BEATS

In this chapter we looked at the first step of the Finding Your Rhythm journey: Step Into Awareness. We discovered the following:

- Being aware helps us control where we're going in life and the rhythm we create.
- When we are unaware, we allow our monkey mind to take us wherever it wishes.
- There are many ways to create awareness, such as

  - meditation,
  - yoga,
  - journaling,
  - listening to and playing music,
  - connecting with nature, and
  - traveling.

With the awareness you've created, you can now join me for the next phase of the Finding Your Rhythm journey and start listening to the rhythm that you have chosen for yourself.

LISTEN TO YOUR RHYTHM

Everything in the universe has a rhythm, everything dances.

—Maya Angelou

Now that you're aware and ready to listen to it, let's find out what your current rhythm is. Is it very fast? Is its speed changing all the time? Does it contain a lot of noisy notes and not many silences? In other words, how are you living your life? What is your life's rhythm?

That's a lot of questions—and answering them requires taking stock of where you are today. Which leads us to more questions. What has been your life's rhythm so far? What experiences led you to where you are now? What are your values? What thoughts have you repeated so often that they became your beliefs? What habits have become part of your daily rhythm? What stories do you tell yourself?

These questions compel introspection, which begins with an honest examination of our egos and emotions. Let's dive in!

YOUR EGO

Let's start with a discussion about ego. Why? As we will discuss, the ego is a strong protector. Although you need a healthy ego to be able to live your life, the protector part can go a step too far and try everything possible to distract you from your true rhythm.

When we are born, we are very connected to our sacred self, our spirit. As children we are still in our purest form, with a heightened spiritual sensitivity. There are many stories about children seeing orbs of light or sparkles—possibly auras or rainbow streaks of energy.[40, 41] Other children have seen spirit entities, such as angels, spirit guides, and other people who have passed away.

In the middle of breakfast a few years ago, my son, who was about three at the time, suddenly said, "Mom, I saw your mother yesterday. She came to visit me. She was very nice!" His grandmother had passed away a year before he was born.

When we're very young and still deeply connected to our spirit, our soul, we are playful, curious, and mostly driven by gut feeling and bodily impulses. But as we get older, we are taught to be more logical. Our rational mind and our thoughts gradually take center stage. The older we get, the more our ego develops. This more protective, practical, and cautious part of ourselves creates a sense of "I"—a sense of being something separate from the world around us.

The world we inhabit has certain norms, certain ways we are supposed to live. We are taught many of them from a very young age: how we should behave, how we should dress, what's considered right or wrong. Many social norms are focused on the development of our ego—not so much on connecting with our spirit, or our true self. These norms are often perpetuated by the people around us, who project their own fears onto our perception of ourselves.

Some people consider ego itself a bad thing—and it can be. I've coached many clients who were overexerting their egos. Their arrogant behavior, driven by fear and scarcity, left them exhausted. But a healthy ego can give us confidence and the willpower to achieve our goals. A healthy ego is life, passion, excitement, growth, drive.

Next time you want to start a new exercise routine or are running a challenging project at work, remember that your ego can help by giving you the will to succeed—just don't let it rule you. As with everything, it's all about balance. As Shahram Shiva—author, writer, poet, recording artist, and award-winning translator and interpreter of Rumi—notes, "Saying ego is bad is as preposterous as . . . water is bad, because it can drown you."[42] He goes on to use hot fire as another example and reminds everyone that water, fire, and ego are life-givers if used correctly.

Spiritual teachings tell us that we live in duality between our ego (our sense of self) and our spirit (our sacred self). The ego is connected to the mind, and whenever it is asked to make a decision, that decision will be based on what the ego knows—the things that have been stored in the mind. In contrast, everything the spirit knows is the universal truth that exists in the present moment, the now. The spirit knows the ways things are, not way we *think* things are. It is where your gut feeling, your intuition, comes from. We have all experienced those situations when, faced with making a decision, we immediately feel what's the right choice for us, and then, within microseconds, our ego comes in and starts mapping the decision against our existing mind maps (a concept we discussed in the introduction). There is nothing right or wrong with either way of decision-making. It is about finding the right balance between your ego and your spiritual self.

When our ego and spirit are out of balance, we often feel confused. Stuck. Out of sync. When our ego's development outpaces that of our spirit, a gap will form. If we don't correct it, it will become wider and wider (see Figure 3). Our self-image grows more and more distant from who we truly are.

Eventually, the gap between our ego self and our spiritual self becomes too wide. We start feeling out of place, stuck, disconnected. *Why am I doing all these things? Is this the life I was meant to live?* These are just a couple of the questions that will come up in this phase, when we've lost sight of who we are.

People react differently to this inflection point, which I call the **offbeat** moment—when the rhythm just doesn't seem to work. This is the moment when my clients come into a session and say, "I don't understand. I have the house, the car, the money, the job, the status—everything I thought would make me feel happy. Everything I thought would make me feel like I'd achieved something in life. But it doesn't feel that way at all. I feel empty. Stuck. How is that possible?"

This is also the moment when it seems like nothing will ever be enough: "I have to keep my job one more year. Then I can afford to live the life I really want." Unfortunately I've heard many clients repeat that same sentence year after year.

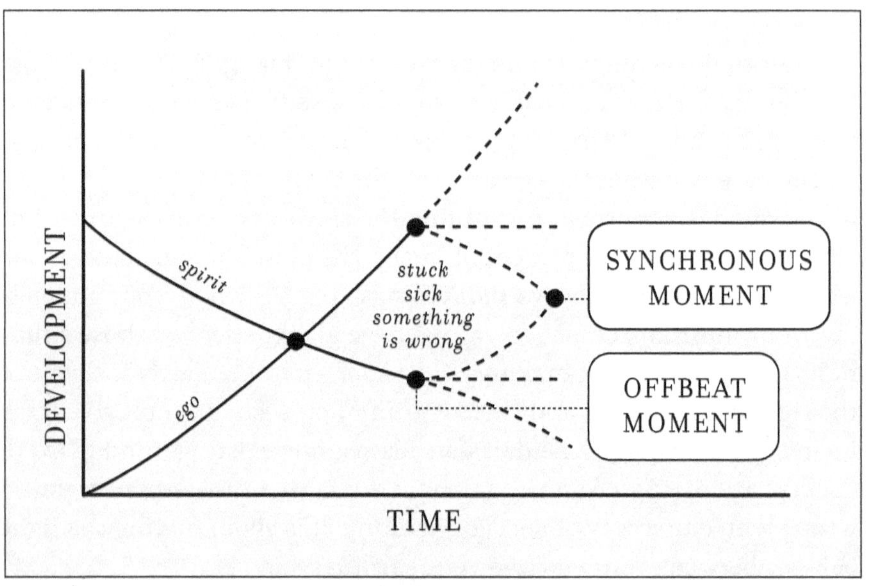

Figure 3. Ego vs. spirit over time—Illustration © Karel Bakkes

Some people are able to keep the gap at a level where it's bearable, which leads to the feeling that you are not really living. It's a bit like the name of that seventies band—Middle of the Road. In this place, you're living a mediocre life, disconnected from your true self. Living this way can lead to all kinds of physical ailments—heart problems, headaches, digestive issues—because you are not addressing the real issue, which is that you aren't living the life you want to lead. You aren't your authentic self. This is not where you want to be.

Other people react to the feeling that something is wrong by focusing even more on their ego. They create a mask for themselves and live their life in denial, completely disconnecting from who they really are.

They often look for refuge in alcohol, drugs, sex, or material things. As you can imagine, this is also not the path to a happy, healthy life.

Then there are the people who do not accept the status quo. Since you picked up this book and are still reading, you are probably one of them! These people experience that offbeat moment and consider it a starting point for personal transformation. They sense the gap and understand that there is more to life. They have faith that their lives will work out. They trust in their capabilities and their inner strength, and they start a journey to let go of their old beliefs, focusing on what's important to them and pointing themselves toward the path of spiritual growth. When the ego and spirit connect again, that's where the magic happens. That's where we are fully in sync.

THE EIGHT DIMENSIONS OF WELLNESS

To really hear our life rhythm, we need to take stock of where we are now—what I call the **As-Is** situation. I usually start the coaching process with a new client with a discussion around the eight dimensions of wellness, presented as a **wellness wheel**. This wheel helps shed light on how we're feeling about the most important things in our life:

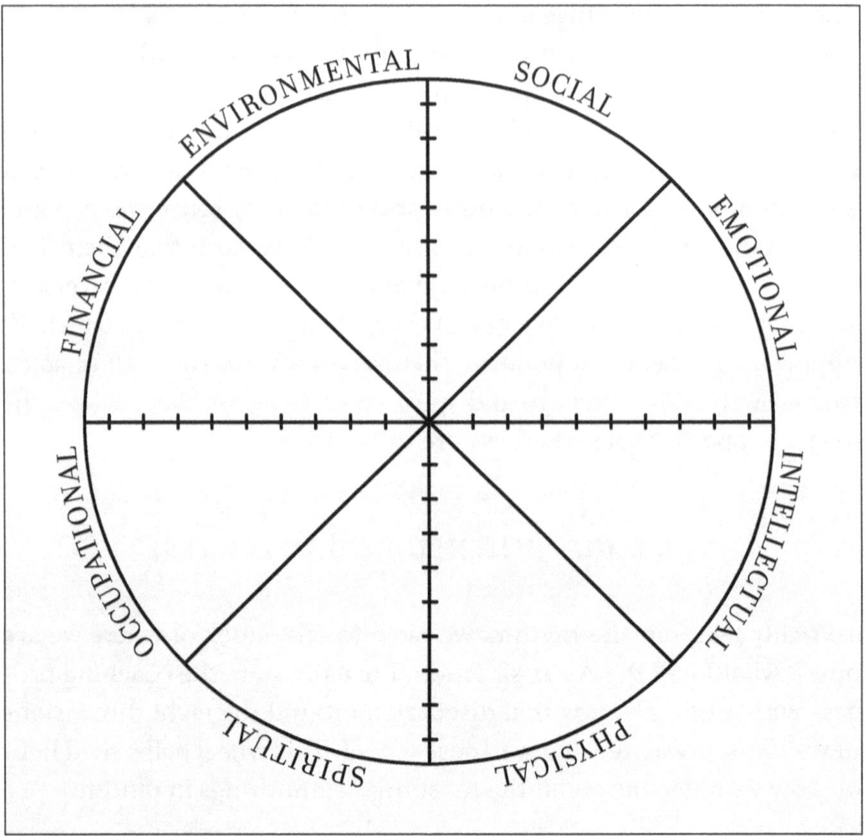

Figure 4. The eight dimensions of wellness

NOTE: The six-dimensional model of wellness is credited to Dr. Bill Hettler in 1976. This eight-dimensional model was developed by University Health Service at the University of Michigan in 2012.

It's critical to carefully assess these dimensions of wellness, because they offer insight into our whole-body health. When one or more parts are not being fulfilled, the deficiency can cause imbalance. And an imbalance in your well-being—be it physical, mental, or spiritual—can make it hard to find your rhythm. But before you evaluate your personal wellness wheel, let's take a brief look at each dimension.

Social

Humans are social beings; we need to feel as if we are part of something, part of a tribe. Whether it's the family tribe, the New York Yankees tribe, the work tribe, or whatever tribe feels like ours, we thrive when we are part of a group.

In his book *Lost Connections*, Johann Hari researched the causes of anxiety and depression, which are abundant in today's world.[43] The number two cause he describes is "disconnecting from other people." We need people around us to share our experiences, our feelings, our emotions, our stories. Yet the way we have organized our world has moved us away from real connection. We live in our own apartments and houses behind closed doors and judge the quality of our social lives by the number of friends we have on social media or by how many "likes" we receive on our most recent posts. How many of us truly take the time to get to know the other people living on our street or in our apartment building—or even our colleagues at work?

Getting expelled from a group causes significant stress—and there's a logical reason for that. The prehistoric part of our brain still reacts to circumstances as it always did. Our ancestors needed the protection of a group; that's how they survived. If they weren't part of a group, they were in trouble. And just as it would have then, when we experience social isolation now, our amygdala goes into overdrive and we mistakenly believe we're in real danger, resulting in adrenaline pumping, heart beating, irrational thinking.

Modern examples of being expelled from a group include sudden situations such as being laid off, going through a divorce, or having friends exclude you. But there is also a *slow* version of group expulsion. For example, if you relocate regularly for your job, you may intend to stay connected to your friends, but it might not always turn out that way. As you build a new life in each new home, you might still talk to your old friends every now and again, but the real connections fade. The in-depth discussions you used to have slowly become more superficial. When you move to a different place every few years, you may have many friends, but the strength of your social network might diminish each time you relocate. I have coached many expat clients who struggle with this. They enjoy the thrill of moving to new environments, have met many people, and probably have a huge number of Facebook friends all over the world, yet they feel increasingly lonely. They long for *real* connection.

So how do we make sure we have a high social wellness level? The key is to work at it; it's not something that can be cultivated by binge-watching your favorite Netflix series or scrolling through your Facebook feed. Social wellness involves openly communicating feelings, needs, and thoughts to those we trust—and actively listening with empathy when feelings, needs, and thoughts are shared. It involves interacting with people who are respectful, positive, and supportive, and maintaining the connection. It comes with intention, effort, and time. Here are some ideas:

- **Schedule a once-a-week outreach.** Go through your contacts list and make a habit of contacting at least one friend a week. Whether you call, text, or send a handwritten letter, maintaining connections is an extremely important part of social wellness.
- **Take up a group hobby**. Find like-minded people who share your interests by joining a hiking club, a community garden, a knitting circle, a writer's workshop, or a painting class. Hobbyists enjoy talking about their craft, so tailor initial discussions to those topics.
- **Join a gym, yoga, fitness, or dance class.** Make small talk before or after. Ask, "How long have you been coming here? What do you like most about it?"
- **Attend an event.** Find interesting events on meetup.com, even if they're a little bit out of your comfort zone. Have an open mind. If you don't like it, you can always leave.
- **Bridge the years.** Reach out to someone you have not spoken to in a long time. Handwritten letters or phone calls will make the experience more intimate.
- **Follow through on synchronous moments**. I believe there's a good reason when someone pops up in your thoughts. Just make the call when that happens!

Of course, this is not an exhaustive list, but I hope it gives you inspiration to build a fulfilling social network. Speaking of social networks, let's talk about the kinds of social circles you might want to avoid. At the top of the list is social media. I do not care how many followers you have on Facebook, Instagram, Twitter, or TikTok; these outlets do not create social wellness. In fact, they create a lot of anxiety. People post only what they want others to see, creating a public facade that rarely reflects their real experiences or feelings. So while Susan might be pictured having dinner on the beach with all her friends, she may actually be struggling with worries about having recently lost her job.

Another unsatisfying way to network socially is at work. Although your job site can seem like a great place to build relationships, it is rife with ethical and legal pitfalls. It can be difficult to share private information, for example, when it could be used against you in meetings or keep you from advancing in your career.

Suppose you have been working hard to get a promotion to regional manager, and you're up against an equally qualified candidate. Things at work are going great, but you're going through some difficult times in your personal life, and you feel the urge to get some of it off your chest. Would you feel comfortable mentioning your personal problem to your colleagues? Probably not, as it could potentially impact the work environment or others' perception of your readiness to do the job. All other things being equal, that detail could tip the scale toward the other candidate. So you remain silent. The result is that many relationships at work remain superficial.

Finally, you do not need to hang on to social relationships that don't support you for who you are. Relationships with toxic people suck up your energy and don't offer anything positive in return. If someone in your social network is *not* respectful, positive, or supportive, it's time to let them go. The next exercise will show you how to do just that.

Letting go means coming to the realization that some people are part of your history, but not part of your destiny.

> ## *EXERCISE*
> ### *CREATE A SOCIAL SCORECARD*
>
> It's important to take an inventory of your social circle periodically. People—including you—change over time, as do their priorities and circumstances. What (or who) was important to you five years ago may no longer be important to you now.
>
> Make a scorecard by listing the names of everyone in your social network. Consider longtime friends, new friends, coworkers, neighbors, classmates, and so forth. For each person, ask yourself two questions:
>
> 1. *Does this person support my vision for how I would like to live my life?*
> 2. *Does this person give me energy, or drain my energy?*
>
> If people do not support you and give you energy, let them go. And by that I mean consciously limit the amount of time you spend with them. Set clear boundaries. Ensure that on most days, you spend the majority of your time with the people who make you feel supported and energized.

Emotional

Emotional wellness is *not* about being happy. Yes, you read that right. Happiness is not the master key to our locker of emotions. In fact, research has found that people who experience various emotions over time, or "emo-diversity," are happier than people who are focused only on finding happiness, no matter the situation.[44] Higher emo-diversity scores are linked to better health. So no, emotional wellness is not just about joy at all costs!

Have you seen the Pixar movie *Inside Out*? If you haven't, please do. In the movie, the five major emotions—Joy, Sadness, Fear, Anger, and Disgust—are personified and reside in the brain of a girl named Riley. The ways the emotions affect Riley and her behaviors are consistent with what science tells us about our feelings, according to an article in *Greater Good* magazine.[45] Moreover, the fundamental messages in the movie are consistent with what we know about positive psychology:

- Happiness is not just about joy.
- Happiness can't be forced.
- Sadness is vital to our well-being.
- Tough emotions should be mindfully embraced rather than suppressed.

Let's look at each message.

Happiness is not just about joy. Many people believe that happiness means being positive all the time. In the world of social media, for example, it's tempting to equate happiness with a news feed full of joyful moments. But think about it: How can we know happiness if we haven't known sadness? Remember when we spoke about rhythm? It consists of a sound and a silence. If it were all sound, it would just be noise. If it were all silence, you wouldn't hear anything. The contrast makes rhythm what it is, and it's the same with happiness. Yes, moments of joy contribute to happiness. But experiencing less-joyful moments creates the contrast you need for a clearer perspective on your overall state. Happiness is the state of being satisfied and content with where you are in life.

Happiness can't be forced. If you make "happiness" your ultimate goal in life, there's a significant chance that striving for it will make you miserable. In a 2011 study, researchers wanted to learn whether there are wrong ways to pursue happiness.[46] What they found is that the more people pursue happiness, the less likely it is that they will actually be happy. What do we do when we pursue happiness? We set goals. And many times, these goals are based on high standards that we derive from, for example, the happy moments our friends share on social media. If we fail to reach our goal, we will feel unhappy. And in the meantime, we forget to enjoy the journey we're on—we are not in the present moment. Many religions, including Buddhism, Christianity, Hinduism, and Bahaism, teach that all frustration, anxiety, and unhappiness come from being overly attached to something. The researchers found that instead of directly pursuing happiness, participating in activities for the activities themselves and not being attached to certain outcomes leads to a much greater likelihood of being happy.

Sadness is vital to our well-being. Sadness helps connect us to people. Whether you experience a death in the family, a divorce, or even just a disappointing grade in school, sadness comes to visit—and there is nothing abnormal about that. It's really important to feel the sadness. Without awareness of that emotion, it's hard to address it; it will stay beneath the surface for a long time—until it becomes too much to carry. When you communicate this sadness to others, it elicits compassion and empathy, creating a connection between you. Connection to others is a very important element in our overall well-being. Sadness also reveals what's important or precious to us, acting as a trigger for growth and change.

Tough emotions should be mindfully embraced rather than suppressed. When you ignore, push away, or suppress difficult feelings, they don't actually go away. They simmer just below the surface. They are waiting for you to notice them; when you don't, they tend to pop up when you least expect it—perhaps as an angry outburst or tears of sadness, seemingly out of nowhere. So when you feel a strong emotion coming on, try to experience it. Try not to judge it or dwell on it. It's OK to feel the emotion; it will pass. Just like you are not your thoughts, you are not your emotions.

EXERCISE

SIT WITH YOUR EMOTIONS

In this exercise, you're going to observe an emotion—just watch it and feel it. I know, doing this is not easy, and it takes practice. Try it with whatever emotion you are feeling right now; then try it again later with stronger emotions.

1. Sit in a comfortable position and close your eyes. Do you feel any emotion coming to the surface? Which emotion is it? Identify it.
2. Invite the emotion to sit down on a chair opposite you. What does the emotion look like? How does the emotion make you feel? What is its color?
3. Give the emotion a name.
4. Observe the emotion. Does being with it nonjudgmentally reduce any anxiety that might normally come up when it visits? Continue to watch it. As the Beatles sang years ago, just "let it be." Don't ignore or suppress the emotion, and know that it will pass.
5. Welcome the emotion by name the next time it visits, and repeat these steps until the feeling passes.

Some other practical tips to increase your emotional wellness are to practice meditation (see Step 1) and to seek help or support from close friends when you're struggling with tough emotions. You might also journal (also described in Step 1), which can help you sort out your feelings in the first place. If you are struggling with improving your emotional wellness and fear you may be stuck in a depressed mood, reach out to a licensed therapist.

Intellectual

The barometer of our intellectual wellness is our openness to learning. We are intellectually healthiest when we can be open to new experiences, when we're curious and embrace the idea of lifelong learning. As Henry Ford said, "Anyone who stops learning is old, whether at twenty or eighty. Anyone who keeps learning stays young."

To support learning, we need to become proficient at three things: mental fitness, sleep, and single-point focus.

MENTAL FITNESS

Keeping the brain fit means forming new neural connections. That's called **brain training**, and it's just as important as physical exercise. When I ran my first half marathon (I'm still working on the full one), I had a stringent training plan. I trained my muscles through regular running and strength exercises, and I combined this with regular rest days and a balanced nutritional plan. We need to do the same for our mental fitness!

So what are some things you can do to keep your brain active and healthy? Simply put, try something new. New things force your brain to be active.

Of course, there are many brain-training apps that you can download on your phone. These can absolutely help, especially if you enjoy the exercises that they offer, which usually test things like focus, math, comprehension, and other mental skills.

Or skip the apps and build one or more of the following activities into your weekly routine:

- **Read a book,** preferably one you wouldn't normally read. Choose a topic or genre that you're unfamiliar with.
- **Go to a museum** and challenge yourself to slow down. Limit yourself to just a few rooms so you can really take in what's on display, not superficially but more deeply.
- **Listen to TED Talks.** Make it a habit to select a TED Talk about a topic that triggers your curiosity.
- **Learn a foreign language.** Choose one that a friend or neighbor speaks so you'll have someone to practice with.
- **Learn to play a musical instrument.** Like learning a foreign language, this is not easy at first, but once you get over the initial hurdle, it's a great ongoing way to stimulate your brain.

Consider coming up with a schedule to embed these activities in your life, but don't forget to also change up your routine periodically. Flip the order around. Swap too-familiar activities with brand-new ones.

Remember when we spoke about rhythm? When rhythm is constant and unchanging, it can become boring, and you can even stop hearing it. When the rhythm changes, your brain is triggered; it recognizes that something new is happening. That's when the working part of your brain becomes active again.

SLEEP

Sleep is also important for your intellectual well-being. Research shows that the brain functions best when it gets at least seven hours of sleep.[47] Revisiting our marathon analogy, the brain needs some rest in addition to the training.

Many of us have trouble falling asleep; our minds are so busy that it's hard to turn off the chatter. When we can't sleep, we get anxious. *It's already 3:00 a.m. and I need to get up at 6:00 a.m. And I have a very important presentation tomorrow. Oh no. I'll look tired, and I probably won't be able to respond quickly to questions because I'm exhausted.* And the chatter continues, making us more anxious and further reducing our chances of falling asleep.

A key factor in getting a good night's sleep is making sure you take the time to wind down. When my clients have difficulty sleeping, I suggest that they block the last hour of the day as sleep-preparation time. One of the most critical steps, albeit challenging for some, is to avoid any screens (phones, tablets, computers, TV) in that last hour.

During the first thirty minutes, think about the things you need to do tomorrow and write them down. It does not have to be a to-do list for the full day, but note the things you don't want to forget to do. These are the things that typically roam around in your head when you go to bed; by writing them down, you've safely stored them and can release them from your thoughts.

During the last thirty minutes, you can read, relax, listen to calming music, practice a breathing exercise, or meditate. If these things do not get you where you want to be, make an appointment with a sleep expert, who should be able to support you in creating a personal sleep plan to ensure you get the sleep you need.

SINGLE-POINT FOCUS

Please forget about multitasking when you're trying to learn something. No matter how many times we tell ourselves we are really good at multitasking, we are not. We just can't split our focus across different activities.

Don't take my word for it: according to an article published in the *Chicago Tribune*,[48] multitasking causes a greater drop in IQ than smoking pot or losing a night's sleep! Please remember this the next time you try to text while driving.

Physical

Do you have a regular exercise routine? What do your eating habits look like? Are you getting enough sleep? Are you receiving preventative medical and dental care? Are you managing your stress? How healthy is your sex life?

These are all important elements for your physical well-being. I know, covering all those bases isn't easy. But I can assure you that taking care of your physical health will have a significant positive impact on your overall well-being. Let's take a closer look at three elements: your exercise routine, your sex life, and your eating habits.

EXERCISE

When I discuss exercise with my clients, I often get questions about types of exercise and intensity, but the main topic that comes up is how to get started. By the time they decide to work with me, people have usually tried many times to start exercise routines but failed to follow through. Even though we know that exercise is vital for our health, we just can't seem to keep or even get it going. So what's the trick? How can you start an exercise routine and make it stick?

It turns out that there are several things you can do to work out smarter, not just harder, and make it a habit. Here's what I've learned from research, along with tips from some of my clients, about successfully starting and maintaining a regular exercise routine:

Choose an exercise that you enjoy: The good thing about moving your body is that there are dozens (maybe hundreds) of ways to do it. The bad thing is that the options can be overwhelming. There are many forms of exercise to choose from—almost too many. Browsing the internet in search of interesting exercise options can easily become overwhelming: running, swimming, cycling, weight lifting, Pilates, yoga, walking, tai chi, aerobics, and the list goes on. So how do you pick? There are a few things to consider. The first, most important question to ask yourself is whether the exercise appeals to you. Is it something you think you will enjoy doing? Is it something you could stick with for a period of time? If you haven't done any regular exercise before, it might be hard to know; the only way to find out is to try.

One note of caution though: Don't try an exercise for only a week. If you want to try something new, find a coach or trainer to support you. For example, if you would like to start swimming but have not had swimming lessons before, or if it's been a long time, find an instructor who can teach you the basic techniques, and then stick to it for at least a month. Why? A new form of exercise takes time to get used to. If you don't learn the right techniques, you risk injuries. But you also risk losing motivation, because you probably will not see a lot of progress right out of the gate. Learning proper technique can feel time-consuming in the beginning, but invest the time in getting the basics right. During my first golf lesson, there were so many things to think about: the grip, the position of your fingers, the stance, the way you swing, your balance, the way you hold your head and where you look when you swing. It was really frustrating at first, but when the techniques started to become more natural after I'd been practicing for some time, that's when the fun started. So don't give up before the fun starts. Give it time.

What if your preferred activity is also something you believe you're bad at? Don't give up! Because if you really enjoy doing something, you will be more likely to stick to it. Returning to the swimming example, if you enjoy being in the water but feel uncoordinated or have a hard time with a certain stroke, hire an instructor or seek out a stroke clinic. Focus on improving one technique at a time. A small adjustment to your kick, your breathing, or the angle of your wrist could make a huge difference in your performance and enjoyment.

The second important question is, How does your chosen exercise fit with your reason for wanting to get more active? Do you want to exercise to help you stay fit and lower your blood pressure? Or do you want to work on flexibility and strength? Or all of the above? Pinpointing your purpose will also help you choose something that you enjoy *and* that serves your needs.

Include different forms of exercise in your routine: People who have been successful in maintaining a good exercise routine often do not limit themselves to one type of workout. Think about how you can build a routine that includes cardio (walking, running, etc.) and some strength and flexibility exercises (weight lifting, yoga, etc.). Varying your activities limits your risk of injury and also decreases the chance that you'll become bored doing the same workout every time.

Set goals that are s-t-r-e-t-c-h-e-d but not unrealistic: Setting goals is important. If you don't set goals for yourself, you'll find it much harder to find the motivation to continue training and improving. But make your goals realistic; they should be something you would really like to achieve, but they should not be overwhelming. If you set them too high, you run the risk of bailing out as soon as you realize they're unattainable. If you set them too low, you probably won't see results soon enough, which can be demotivating. I suggest working with a coach or trainer, if possible, to ensure that your goals are aligned with the objectives of your exercise.

Stick to the plan: People often are very enthusiastic when they start exercising and feel they can do much more than what their workout plan suggests. One of my clients started with the objective of having more energy and feeling more fit. The first step he wanted to take was to train to run a 5K in thirty minutes. He had not exercised for many years, so the program his running coach suggested started with three to four weekly walks/runs at a really slow pace, with 250 meters running and 750 meters walking. Not really liking the pace, my client ran five or six days, and longer distances than recommended. Initially he felt great, but after only two weeks he injured his calf muscles. The result was two months' recovery time, with no walking or running.

Get a coach: Work with a personal trainer or coach if you can afford to do so, to make the most of your time and effort. A coach can set up an exercise plan based on your fitness objectives, monitor your progress, and help you stay motivated. These days many coaches can do a lot online, so there's no need to physically be together for every session. For example, when I started training for the Auckland half marathon, I worked with a coach I saw only once every few months. The rest of the time, he monitored my progress through the data I collected with my Garmin watch. Based on the data, he would adjust my training plan on a weekly basis.

Use technology: Today's technology and the resulting data can help you avoid injuries, enjoy exercising, and improve your fitness level. There are tools to track your progress in almost any sport. Of course, it's important to listen to your body first and your exercise technology second (don't do it the other way around; I made that mistake). The first piece of technology I recommend is a heart rate monitor. You can get a lot of guidance from just measuring your heart rate: Your resting heart rate is a good indication of your fitness level, and when you start exercising, you will slowly see your resting heart rate drop, which is always a good motivator. When you see your heart rate going up or you wake up with a very high resting heart rate, your heart could be telling you that you're coming down with something, you're overtraining . . . or you're just hungover.

The other reason for using a heart rate monitor is that it helps you focus on the intensity level of your workouts. When you start training, it's good to build up your fitness by exercising slowly for a period of time, keeping your heart rate below 65 percent of its maximum rate; this is the zone where you burn fat and build fitness. A simple way to calculate your maximum heart rate is 220 minus your age. So, if you are forty-five, your maximum heart rate is 175. Try to do this for some time until you have built up a good level of fitness. Subsequently you can start adding some aerobic (cardio) training into the mix.

One truly fantastic platform is TrainingPeaks (TrainingPeaks .com). It connects to many exercise watches and can give you good insight into how you are improving your fitness, and warn you of possible overtraining by measuring your fatigue level. It can also connect to your coach, who can analyze your progress and update your training plan remotely.

SEX LIFE

"Do you have a healthy sex life?" my coach asked. I thought it was a rather intrusive question, and I also was not really sure what my sex life had to do with my coaching topic. I had told him I wanted to discuss why I felt I was losing interest in or passion for my work. I tried dodging the question, but being the coach he was, he did not give up; he explained that a healthy sex life is a fundamental part of overall well-being.

In a study done in 2015,[49] researchers found a strong correlation between frequency of sexual activity and our overall well-being. Especially for people in committed relationships, regular sexual contact has an impact both on the relationship and on each partner's psychological, physical, and overall health.

How does an active sex life relate to physical well-being? An article published by VerywellMind.com reported a number of physical benefits from regular sexual activity, including better physical fitness, enhanced brain function, improved immune function, lower pain levels, weight loss, improved cardiac health, healthier teeth, better digestion, and glowing skin.[50] With this long list of benefits, who wouldn't want to schedule frequent visits to the bedroom (or another location of choice)? Unfortunately, having a healthy sex life can sometimes take a little work; a lack of intimacy is still one of the main reasons relationships end.[51] Although a discussion about how to revitalize your sex life, or how to develop a healthy one, goes beyond the scope of this book, I encourage you to keep an open mind. Many of my clients are reluctant to discuss their sex life, but since it can affect your well-being significantly, I would advise you to start the conversation with your partner if you feel there is room for improvement—and, if needed, seek the help of a sex therapist.

NUTRITION

Did you know that your body rejuvenates itself completely every seven to ten years?[52] Perhaps even more surprising is that many parts of the body change a lot more frequently than that. For example, your skin cells rejuvenate every two to four weeks, and the cells that line the surface of the stomach and intestines cycle every five days. Your skeletal system changes constantly, although the complete renewal takes up to ten years. In order to rebuild, your body needs nutrients: proteins, fats, carbohydrates, vitamins and minerals, and water. All these nutrients have specific functions for maintaining and rebuilding the body.

Nutritional needs vary from person to person: if you are a professional athlete, your needs will be different than those of someone who sits behind a desk all day. In addition to your activity level, many other factors play a role in determining your nutritional needs, including gender, body type, and age. There are various ways to determine what your body needs, the simplest of which is to identify your basal metabolic rate (BMR) using an online calculator and, with that info, find your suggested caloric intake. (Your BMR basically gives you the number of calories you'd burn if you stayed in bed all day.) Another option is to use one of the many nutrition-tracking apps available. But if you want to take a more personalized approach and learn more about foods and diet, the best thing to do is consult a nutrition specialist, who can ensure that your plan is fully aligned with your unique requirements.

Many people try specific diets to boost their nutritional intake and, of course, to lose weight. But diets often aren't healthy, and some may not meet your nutritional needs. In addition, many weight-loss programs cause people to shed pounds pretty quickly—and then bounce back to their old weight not too long after completing the program. Why? Because fad diets are purposefully designed to fail. It is estimated that the weight-loss and weight-management industry is worth between USD 400 billion and 450 billion globally!

To bring about long-term change, you need to look at your overall lifestyle and make slow, gradual adjustments. For example, if you want to start eating a vegetarian diet, begin with two or three meatless days per week, see how your body reacts, and adjust accordingly. Vegetarian diets are healthy for some people but not for everyone. Always check with your healthcare provider before starting a new eating plan.

Maybe you were intrigued, as I was, by the documentary *Gamechangers*,[53] which showed high-level athletes changing to a vegan diet and improving their performance. Does this mean you should change to a vegan diet too? Not necessarily. It's important to remember that the wisdom on what's "healthy" changes over time. For many years we were told that eating steak would make us strong and powerful and would help us perform at a high level. But is that really true—or was it good marketing? Just like the ads for the sugar-loaded sodas that were promoted to our children for years. Research had already shown that sugar, especially the level found in soda, was toxic. Yet we kept on promoting the supersized bottles for years!

More and more people are becoming aware of the falsehoods embedded in flashy marketing campaigns and food trends and are starting to make their own informed decisions about what they eat. The Covid pandemic propelled us all to be more mindful about eating healthy food. As a result, there has been a significant increase in people who are interested in and switching to plant-based diets.

If you want to nourish your body while also stimulating your brain with a new way of thinking about food, take some time to learn about Ayurveda. In the Ayurvedic way of eating, you consume mainly whole or minimally processed food, and you make food choices based on your dominant *dosha* (energy type). It is not a one-size-fits-all plan, but is instead tailored to you—your constitution, energy level, body type, and habits. In addition to providing guidance on what to eat based on your unique needs, Ayurvedic practices also focus on mindful eating, quantity of food consumed, and ideal timing of meals.

Ayurveda has been around a long time, by some accounts more than five thousand years, stemming from ancient Vedic culture in India. Its dietary practices are only one part of a holistic system of health care.

Spiritual

There are many different views on what spirituality and spiritual health mean. For the purposes of this book, I define spirituality as a deep sense of being and interconnectedness. "A deep sense of being" refers to being at peace with yourself, grounded, and empathetic. The "interconnectedness" piece could refer to your connection with yourself, others, or your environment. Exploring your spiritual core—your purpose, your values, your beliefs—is critical for improving your spiritual health. Following a religious faith can be part of spiritual health, especially when it is fulfilling. But for our purposes, I'm most interested in who *you* are. The connection you have to *you*.

In my coaching practice, I often find that high-achieving people are so busy getting things done and managing the lives of those around them that they don't take the time to check in with themselves—to see if their actions are truly aligned with their authentic selves. Remember Peter? Here's how he realized that he'd been neglecting his spiritual health:

Peter: I don't think my current relationship is going anywhere. We're stuck. It used to be an amazing relationship. We felt like soulmates. But somewhere along the line, we lost the connection. My partner is always very negative and never seems satisfied with anything.
Me: Can you give me some examples of when you feel she's not satisfied?
Peter: Sure. It happens all the time. She's been at home with our son since he was born, and now she's trying to get her life back. But everything I do for her ends up going nowhere!
Me: Peter, can you give me an example of something you did for her that made you feel this way?
Peter: Yes, sure! She wanted to build a career as a coach. I supported her with her coaching training. Then she wanted to start building a client base, so I introduced her to people in my corporate network—but she didn't even call them. Or the workshop I developed for her about personal branding: I made the whole presentation and storyline for her and helped her sell it to a first client. But when the day came, she bailed out and I needed to run the workshop for her. And she wanted to have a webshop, so I built it. I spent hours and hours building a webshop. She bought a lot of things she wanted to sell. I asked her to prepare an overview of the items so I could start listing them. That overview never came. We've been paying money for that webshop for years now, but never made a penny!

Me: How does that make you feel, Peter?

Peter: Angry. Frustrated. She doesn't recognize all the things I do for her. I work very hard in a job I don't really like. For her. So that she can have the life she wants. I built the website so she can start selling and traveling in Asia to buy interesting things to sell. I introduce her to clients. I do everything, but all I get is negativity. She feels depressed and doesn't know what she really wants.

Me: Mmmm . . . And what about Peter? What do *you* want? I hear you talk about all the sacrifices you are making for her, but I have not heard you talk about what you want. Peter, you're the CEO of a company. What would happen if you ran around all day trying to make people happy, but not having a clear vision about where you wanted to go? Who are *you*, Peter? What's your purpose for being in a relationship?

Peter: [*Long silence*] I don't know. I guess I've never really thought about who I want to be in our relationship. I'm struggling right now just to come up with an answer to that question. What do I want? I don't know.

I have seen this scenario over and over again in my practice. We live our lives in such a way that we completely forget about ourselves and our own needs. This is when we start feeling unhappy or stuck in life and blaming our misery on others. To change that, we need to look inward and ask ourselves, *Who am I? What do I want? How do I want to be? What is my purpose?*

Just consider these questions for now. Later in this chapter, we'll look at values and beliefs—and how they define who we are at our core. There, you'll have a chance to explore your own values and beliefs by doing two exercises.

Occupational

If you are struggling to find joy in your job, you're not alone. Many people hate their jobs, and only 15 percent of the global workforce reports being engaged at work.[54] Think about all the time we spend at work. It's a wonder that we don't leave!

The reasons we stay in unfulfilling jobs are often based on old, limiting beliefs, like *I'll never be able to find another job. I'm already too old.* Sometimes it's the fear of starting something new that keeps people in a job they don't like—*What if my boss at the new company is even worse than the one I have now?* And we can continue in this vein for a long time.

In response to fears like these, I like to offer a quote by Erin Hanson, "What if you fall? Oh darling, but what if you fly?"

Another reason people stay in positions that make them unhappy is because these jobs pay the bills, and they believe that they could never achieve the same level of financial security doing something they love. That may be true mathematically, but is it true *spiritually*?

Let me explain. I have assisted many of my clients in overcoming obstacles to pursuing their dreams, particularly dreams related to the question *What do I want to do for a living?* But I have a unique approach. I ask them to completely rethink their objectives rather than just "flipping" them.

Many well-meaning coaches and self-help books tell people to simply flip their old beliefs to new ones. For example, the belief *I can't make the same money I'm making today doing something I love* is flipped to *I can make the same or even more money than I'm making today by doing something I love.* Sounds good, right? But unfortunately, this advice falls short because it follows the same old belief pattern and ignores the bigger picture.

In my practice, I encourage out-of-the-box thinking and make sure my clients' *values* inform their goals. Using the same example from before, I recommend transforming *I can't make the same money I'm making today by doing something I love* to *I can support myself and my family by doing something I love.* The thing is—and this is the big takeaway—if you do what you love, the money becomes less relevant!

Imagine you are someone who loves to travel, but you currently have a high-paying corporate job. You drive to work every day in heavy traffic, and after waving your security badge you get into the elevator and walk to your well-deserved corner office. You work in the marketing department, writing the messages that help sell your company's products. Two times a year you go on an expensive one-week vacation. Even while you are away, though, work continues, and you spend at least one or two hours a day on your phone. You're making the money you were hoping for, but not really doing what you love. Now you get a call from a headhunter who tells you about a job opportunity as a writer for a travel magazine. You would be traveling most of the time, writing about events happening around the world. However, you would make half the money you do today. Would you pass on that?

You might be thinking, *Yeah, there's no way I would work for half my pay. Not a chance. I'd definitely pass.* This hypothetical scenario is not meant to suggest that you can't make the same or more money than you are currently by doing what you love. It's meant to encourage you to notice your limiting beliefs: you went to *I can't* instead of *Well, maybe.* Be careful with your beliefs. If you do what you love, you'll shift where you allocate your time. You'll prioritize what you enjoy. This can lead to other positive changes in all eight dimensions of the wellness wheel. And so it's possible that the dollar amount you think you need is really quite arbitrary.

In order to feel engaged in your work—which, again, only 15 percent of the global workforce experiences—your job must be connected to something bigger than yourself: to your purpose, your meaning in life. Let me give you an example.

Years ago, I was working with an executive at a healthcare company. We met in a local coffee shop across the street from his company's headquarters. He looked a bit tense and not too happy. After we ordered coffees and sat down, I asked him if anything was wrong.

He said, "Yes. I'm frustrated with all the internal politics and our short-term focus on results. I guess we have to have this focus, as a publicly traded company, but it is frustrating."

After further discussion, I asked him why he was still with the company if it was so frustrating. His answer was remarkable and really hit home for me: He explained that five years earlier he had been diagnosed with cancer. As a result of his access to healthcare and the best medical technology, he was completely cured. Afterward, he made a promise to himself that he would do everything possible to help make healthcare available to the millions of people who did not have access to it.

"If I leave the company, sure, I can do many other things, but I will never be able to have the same impact," he explained. "Yes, 25 percent of my time is the b*llsh*t I am now frustrated about. And that's OK.

Because 75 percent of my time, I'm working to make healthcare available to the millions of people who do not have it today."

This was a great lesson for me: In any job, even one you would absolutely love to do (and perhaps already do), there will be tasks that might not be high on your "love-to-do" list. However, if the percentage of those tasks stays below 25 percent, suck it up and focus on the other 75 percent. How can you tell whether you're in a healthy range at your job? Go to http://www.authentes.com/finding-your-rhythm and download the Work Happiness Score Worksheet to determine your satisfaction level.

Financial

Whether or not you are happy with your financial situation depends on two things: how much money you currently have or generate as income, and your beliefs about how much money you need to live a comfortable life.

Almost without exception, my clients tell me that they will be satisfied with their financial wellness if they get the promotion they've always wanted, work for *x* more years, sell the company, or win the lottery (not a good strategy). It's no different whether people have USD 50,000 or 3 million in their bank account, or whether they make USD 80,000 or 500,000 a year. Most people feel like they are "almost there" and just need to save *a little bit* more. In other words, it is never enough.

Financial wellness is all about your relationship with money and how you manage your resources. Having a good understanding of your fiscal situation and taking care of it so that you're prepared for any changes both contribute to financial wellness. It's also important to determine how much money you actually need to be happy.

Years ago, I was on a leadership journey in Tibet. During that trip we visited many monasteries, and at one of them I interacted with someone who lived there. We exchanged some sign-language dialogue, and he showed me the place where he lived. At that time I was living in a big villa with a swimming pool and had just bought a Tesla and a "just for fun" Harley-Davidson. This person did not have any of those things. He lived a room the size of half my study. He had a few items of clothing, a bed, and a stove. But the one thing he did have that

I'd lacked for many years was a smile that radiated happiness! I have included the picture for you to judge.

After that experience, I made some significant changes to my life. I sold the big villa and decided to live more modestly. A year before my journey to Tibet, we had bought a new designer table for our living room. And as you may know, designer furniture does not come cheap. The table was delivered, we put it in the living room, and that was it.

It looked good. But before we knew it, the table was just there and was nothing special. In my new house, I put a table I'd bought from a secondhand store. Together, my son and I sanded it smooth and painted it. It was a fraction of the cost of the designer table and brought me joy every time I saw it. The big lesson for me: money does not make us happy if we are offbeat.

The definition of "enough" money is different for everyone. It depends on what you think life should look like and what makes you truly happy. When people don't have a roof over their head or money for food and clothes, having access to more money is obviously important for their life satisfaction and emotional well-being. Researchers found that having an income between USD 60,000 and 75,000 leads to a high level of emotional well-being, and having an income of USD 95,000 leads to a high level of life satisfaction.[55] Since the study was published in 2018, those number might have changed due to inflation, but in general they are much lower than the income most of my clients say they need to have a happy life. One other interesting finding: when people make more than USD 105,000, their life satisfaction actually decreases!

Environmental

The environment you live in is important, because each environment has a certain rhythm, a certain pace. What rhythm are you looking for? If you love to be out in nature, you probably aren't going to enjoy living in the middle of Sao Paolo. If you love cities, a ranch in the US Midwest is probably not your thing.

When I was living in Beijing, I experienced for the first time how your environment can impact your day-to-day life. Before then I had been living in the Netherlands, where the air quality is some of the best in the world. I had read about the pollution in Beijing but thought, *How bad can it be?* Bad. It can be really bad. My wife and I arrived in Beijing on a very polluted day. We felt assaulted the moment we stepped out of the airplane—headache, sore throat, and fatigue.

We immediately bought air purifiers for our apartment and masks for walking outside. Our son was born a few months later, and the air quality also had a significant impact on him. Teaching a baby to keep a mask on is not easy. And when he was a bit older, he had to stay inside the apartment for at least five or six months of the year because of dangerously high pollution levels. After living in Beijing for about four years, we moved to New Zealand. I don't think we could have found a bigger contrast in air quality!

It's also important to consider your immediate environment, both at home and at work. I found that during the Covid-19 lockdown it was really important for me to keep my apartment clean and tidy. I made it a habit to make the bed and wash the dishes every day, and I cleaned the apartment once a week. When I was writing this book, I always put my computer and any supplies I needed on the kitchen table, where I worked. But after work each day, I would put them away, even though I knew I needed to come back to the same spot the next day. In fact, these habits became even more important to me than they had been before the pandemic. Although it would have been easy to just leave the bed as is, clean the apartment only when really necessary, and leave my computer on the kitchen table—no one was allowed to come in during the lockdown anyway!—it was important to me to minimize clutter and keep a certain rhythm going.

I feel the same way about an office environment. Some people thrive in offices with stacks of paper everywhere. And the interesting thing is that when you ask them for a certain document, they somehow know exactly where to look. I always find that amazing, but it's not an environment I could work in. For most people, decluttering is important. Clearing away the extra stuff screaming for our attention helps us focus, and organizing our work space can result in dramatic changes in lifestyle and perspective.[56]

There are a lot of things to consider when you start evaluating whether your environment is in sync with the rhythm of your life, but they can generally be split into three main categories:

- **Safety and security:** Consider crime rate and exposure to toxins, such as electromagnetic fields and air pollution. Most of all, listen to your gut! We have all had moments when our gut tells us that we are in the wrong place. And our gut is usually right. One caveat though: keep in mind that sometimes your brain plays the safety card when it's not warranted. For example, when I traveled to Asia after a long stint in the Netherlands, my brain had a hard time analyzing what was safe and what wasn't, because everything was unfamiliar. I was definitely out of my comfort zone, so I stayed in close range of my hotel. Many years later, after having lived in Asia, I returned to that same hotel and realized that my brain had been overprotecting me, limiting me to the area around the hotel because that seemed safer. As a result, I had missed out on seeing so many beautiful landscapes and major sights! So yes, do trust your gut feeling. But also ask yourself what you're sensing. Is it your gut giving you a warning sign, or your brain trying to keep you in the comfort zone?

- **Physical comfort:** Consider how your body responds to climate, noise levels, the colors of the natural and man-made landscapes, the availability of green areas or parks, access to transportation, and the furnishings in your home. At conscious and unconscious levels, you react to what you see, hear, and smell in your environment. These stimuli can affect your mood and emotions, and ultimately your health. Even a simple change, such as putting a picture on your desk of a beautiful place you've visited, could lift your mood when you see it.

- **Psychological comfort:** Consider how the community and culture make you feel. Can you rely on the people around you when you need to? Do you share interests with them? What are the social norms of the community? How does your environment support and accept different ideas and different people? Are your beliefs and values welcome and respected? It will be very hard to find your rhythm if your thoughts and priorities don't mesh with your surroundings.

EXERCISE

THE WELLNESS WHEEL

On my website, you can download the Wellness Wheel Worksheet to determine how you're faring in each of the eight dimensions of wellness. The scoring goes from zero to ten, with zero being very dissatisfied with that area of your life and ten being extremely satisfied. Don't try to read too much into the scores right now. We will do that in a later chapter, when we compare your current score to the one you would like to have. I have done many wellness wheel exercises with clients and have seen just as many wellness scores. There is no right or wrong score—it is simply a reflection of where you are right now. Be honest with yourself. If you don't have access to the internet right now, you can record your scores using the following table. Enjoy the exercise!

My Current Scores:

Area	*Current Score*
Social	
Emotional	
Intellectual	
Physical	
Spiritual	
Occupational	
Financial	
Environmental	

Psychometric Analysis

Over the last few decades, psychometric analysis has become a popular personal-development tool. It is meant to give you insights into your current personality profile. I've included psychometric analysis in this book because it provides another perspective on the As-Is situation of your personal rhythm.

What is psychometric analysis? Psychometric testing is intended to measure an individual's mental capabilities and behavioral style. This type of personality profiling has been around for a long time. Twenty-four hundred years ago, Hippocrates suggested that every person has one of the following temperaments: Air, Fire, Earth, or Water. Many of the profiling tools available today are still based on this model.

A multitude of psychometric assessments have been developed over the years. You might have heard about some of them, such as MBTI, Hogan, and Extended DISC. Google "best psychometric assessment" and you'll be surprised by the huge list that appears!

Companies often use psychometric assessments in their hiring process to determine whether specific individuals are the right fit for certain organizational roles. These assessments compensate for human bias in the hiring process. Research done by a large HR consulting firm revealed that the likelihood of a hiring manager making a poor choice is *50 percent*, only *14 percent* of unstructured job interviews predict top talent, and *99 percent* of hires are based on first impressions![57]

How is any of this relevant to your Finding Your Rhythm process? A high-quality assessment can give you a range of insights into your natural behavioral style and how it impacts the people around you.

However, before you start filling out a bunch of questionnaires, there are a few caveats: First, make sure that you use a well-respected and -tested assessment tool; I use either Extended DISC or Hogan assessments in the coaching I do with clients—typically in the beginning of our coaching journey together. Second, please make sure to find a coach or someone who is certified to walk you through the results. Without a good explanation of your assessment report, you might draw the wrong conclusions. Third, remember that the assessments simply give you insights into your preferred or natural behavioral style. There is no right or wrong style! And finally, although the data can be helpful to you, it may also hinder your process of creating change and getting rid of old beliefs if you are not mindful of the risk of confirmation bias. Let me tell you a short story to explain.

Years ago, I was attending a leadership development training session for my new role as office managing partner in one of my firm's larger offices. There were four of us sitting around a square table, and each person had a sign in front of him or her that said either The Clown, The Ignored, The Serious One, or The Expert. We were asked to discuss a certain topic and react to each other based on the signs in front of us. When The Clown started talking, we would laugh or giggle. When The Ignored talked, someone else would talk over him, and we would all pretend he wasn't saying anything. What followed was really interesting. We started to behave in ways that were consistent with how we were treated! The Clown thought he was really funny and started making jokes; The Ignored stopped even trying to say anything because he knew no one was going to listen; The Serious One's responses grew more and more serious; and The Expert felt very well respected and started sharing insights as if she had all the answers.

The risk I want to warn you of is that you may read your assessment report and start behaving accordingly. Let's say that the assessment labels you an introvert. I have seen people convert such information into a limiting belief. For example, you might decide that since you are introverted, you will never be good at sales. That is not helpful!

In a Japanese study, sixty-four females took a popular psychometric test and were given randomly assigned results stating that they were either introverted or extroverted. Then they were asked to interact with strangers. The "extroverted" participants had much more interactive discussions with the strangers than the "introverted" ones. The experiment showed that the outcome of such a test can influence human behavior and create a self-fulfilling prophecy.[58]

In short: Don't use the assessment as an excuse or a limiting belief. Use it as an opportunity to reflect on your current or preferred behavior and how that behavior is helping you achieve your goals.

YOUR LIFELINE

So far in this chapter, you've listened to your rhythm by taking stock of where you are on the eight dimensions of wellness and through psychometric analysis. But how did you get where you are? Why did you create the rhythm you are currently playing in your life? Taking a look at your lifeline can help you gain some insight into these questions.

There's a lot you can learn from plotting the highs and lows of your life on a diagram. A lifeline can give you clues about what you really enjoy doing and what you don't enjoy. It can serve as a map of your values and beliefs (more about that soon). And when you share your lifeline with others, if you feel comfortable doing so, you can deepen your bond with them. A few years ago I participated in a session with the leadership team of a large telecom company in the Netherlands. Members of the team had been working together for a while but had never really taken the time to get to know each other. Coincidentally it was a turbulent time in the telecom industry, and the team had been focusing on one crisis after another. The very first exercise they did was to create lifelines.

They spent thirty minutes working on their own lifelines (see Figure 5)—thinking about significant events, relationships, and places— and then each team member presented theirs to the group. They spoke about personal events from their lives and in doing so created connections with each other that had not existed previously. Over the three days they were together for this session, they reflected back frequently on the events they had shared. The impact on the group was truly amazing.

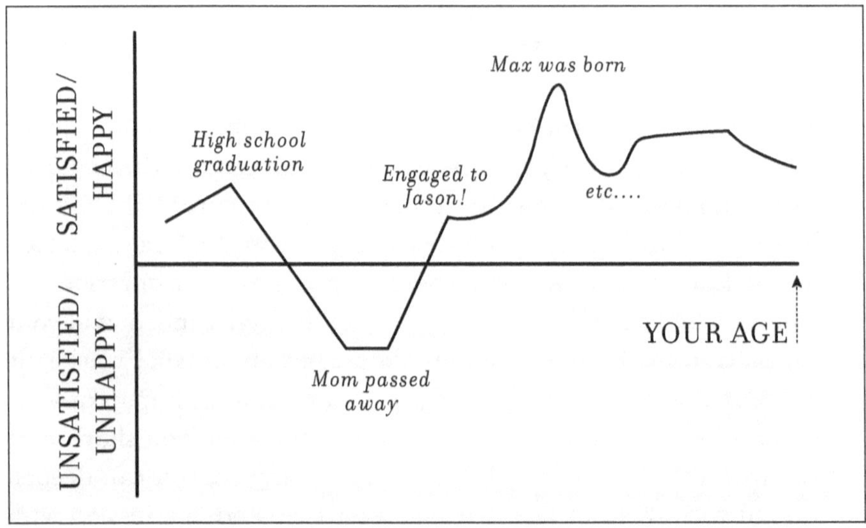

Figure 5. The lifeline

Before you start working on your lifeline, it helps to clear your head. Take several minutes to meditate, go for a brisk walk, take a shower, or do whatever works for you to empty your mind.

EXERCISE
DRAW YOUR LIFELINE

On a blank page of your journal, draw a simple line graph like the example given in Figure 3. Label the vertical line with Unhappy/Unsatisfied at the bottom and Happy/Satisfied at the top. The horizontal line should start when you were born and end at your current age, all the way to the right. Alternatively, go to http://www.authentes.com/finding-your-rhythm and download and print the Lifeline Worksheet.

Plot impactful events, relationships, and places on the graph. Include both positive and negative peak moments—any event that impacted you significantly. Start with your earliest memory, probably around the age of six or seven, and go through your life up until today. You'll probably have no problem recalling the big events, such as graduation, moving away from home, getting married, or the death of a loved one. But also try to remember minor moments that nevertheless impacted your life or your outlook on it, such as something kind someone did for you, a scare you had while traveling, or the exhilarating feeling when you were first introduced to someone or something you now love.

After all the events have been plotted, connect the dots to create your lifeline.

Next, write about each event in your journal or on the worksheet. Describe what happened. Write about how each event impacted the ones that followed it.

The last step is to reflect on this exercise. Looking back on your life, ask yourself which events impacted you most significantly, and why. If an event resulted in a period where you were not happy, what did you do to turn your life around?

Do you see any patterns? What can you take away from looking at your life like this? Are there any obvious attributes of the happy moments that you can bring forward to how you want to live your life? Are there any common attributes of the unhappy moments that you can avoid?

In case you're struggling with what to plot on your timeline, here's an example from my life. Years ago, I was on a business trip to Florida. I had a three-day event in Orlando, a long weekend in between, and then another event in Fort Lauderdale. It was during a time in my life when I was a bit stuck and unsure about what I wanted to do. I had a decent job and was making good money, but I was not happy. I wasn't living the life I had envisioned for myself, and I wasn't sure how to change that. That weekend, I decided to rent a motorcycle and drive to Key West. I went to the Harley-Davidson dealer and rented a big touring machine. I loved it. It had been a long time since I'd ridden a motorcycle like that! When I turned on the engine, I felt it: freedom. The ride was fantastic. I rode for hours, crossing the Seven Mile Bridge and seeing many beautiful spots. In Key West I had a few drinks in a bar and a great dinner. I met a few people, and I felt freer than I had in a long time. That trip made me realize how important freedom is to me. As a result, on my lifeline, the brief jaunt to Key West is one of my peak moments; it had a significant impact on how my lifeline would continue.

BELIEFS

Your lifeline shows you the moments that had a significant impact on you or touched you in important ways. It provides a good overview of how your life has progressed so far. But what is the driving force behind all of this? What factors came into play when you were making choices in your life? What is the force that actually created your rhythm?

Beliefs are thoughts that we have elevated to a higher level. These are not just random thoughts that come and go. No, beliefs are thoughts we consider to be absolutely true. However, they don't necessarily have to be true! Facts are facts—they are true and can be verified as such. That is not always the case for our beliefs.

Our beliefs are formed at a very young age as we observe the things around us. We watch our parents, our teachers, our peers, the media, and figures from popular culture. We form so many ideas based on our environment that we even embrace beliefs that are not our own!

We carry those beliefs with us as we become adults, and we rely on them when we make decisions. To do this, our brain is constantly trying to link those old beliefs we've stored to what is happening in the present. Unfortunately, these cached beliefs do not include much detail, and sometimes a situation can be falsely tied to a belief. I like to compare them to low-resolution photographs in which the objects pictured could easily be mistaken for something completely different. The behaviors or actions that result from our old beliefs could be completely misaligned with what is truly happening in the moment.

In addition, our beliefs can be so pervasive that we take them as fact, even when they prevent us from growing or being our true selves.

These are called **limiting beliefs**. Here are some examples of limiting beliefs that we tell ourselves:

- *I can't make money doing what I love.*
- *I will never be able to lose weight.*
- *I am too old to quit my job and start doing what I love.*
- *I will never find someone who will love me for who I am. When people really get to know me, they will realize that I'm boring.*
- *I cannot meditate. As soon as I sit down, my thoughts start distracting me—it will never work.*

Do you recognize some of these beliefs? How many of them are facts? How many of these beliefs could you actually verify to be true?

It's not surprising that, consciously or not, we embrace beliefs that are not ours. From advertisements we believe we have to look a certain way. From Hollywood movies we believe we have to act a certain way. From society we form our beliefs about where it's safe to be and who it's safe to be around. From our parents and other influential adults, we form beliefs about what jobs, hobbies, and lifestyles are acceptable.

But living your life based on beliefs that are not yours will lead you to becoming stuck, unhappy, or depressed. *What the hell is going on?* you'll think. You'll believe you were doing everything right, but what you're doing just won't feel good. A lot of these limiting beliefs are hard to access. They are there, but at an unconscious level.

An important step is excavating them, and that's not easy!

EXERCISE
YOUR LIMITING BELIEFS

Grab your journal and a pen. (Or download and print the Beliefs Worksheet from http://www.authentes.com/finding -your-rhythm.) Sit down where you'll be undisturbed for at least fifteen minutes. For each question, write down five to ten beliefs you have. Don't worry about whether the beliefs are "good" or "bad," or whether they are yours or someone else's. Just write them down nonjudgmentally. Need ideas? Here are some questions for inspiration:

- What are some of the things you tell yourself that are not very loving?
- What have you always struggled with? What do you believe you are bad at?
- What do you think is wrong with you?
- Review your lifeline. Do you notice any limiting beliefs when you review your significant events?

Now look over your answers, and consider which beliefs are holding you back. These are your limiting beliefs, the ones that may be making you feel stuck, unhappy, uncomfortable, or anxious. Identify your top five to ten limiting beliefs and write them down.

If you're still struggling to identify your limiting beliefs, please visit my website. Under Resources I have included a sample list of 101 limiting beliefs—enough to get you started!

Once you're aware of your limiting beliefs, you'll start seeing their impact on your daily decisions. These beliefs have been with you for a long time, so they won't just disappear. That's where working with a coach—and understanding your values—can be really helpful.

In the following section on values, you'll learn how to convert limiting beliefs into beliefs that will help you create the life you want to live!

VALUES

Your values are another invisible force that controls your decisions and your direction in life. The life you're living today is a result of the decisions you've made. When you explore where you are in life, you are unconsciously comparing the life you lead with how in sync your life and values are.

Let me give you an example. Let's just imagine that freedom is one of your values. A nine-to-five government job, where you are told each day which project to work on, is probably not going to score very high for freedom. If security were one of your main values, that might be the right job for you.

The other thing to realize about values is that the order in which you prioritize them is important. If, with the last example, freedom and security were both on your list of values, you would probably make that job choice based on whichever value had the higher priority.

So where do these values come from? In our early years, between ages zero and seven, our values develop mainly unconsciously, through what we learn from our parents and caregivers. After that, as we do with our core beliefs, we consciously and unconsciously copy some of the values of the people around us, like our friends, teachers, and neighbors. Many of our core values were formed by the time we were ten years old, so they've been with us for a long time!

When these values are truly our own, we behave in ways that align with our authentic selves. But remember our discussion about the formation of our beliefs, and how some of them are adopted from others? The same is true with values. Sometimes we adopt those of the people around us, unconsciously copying whatever values *they* live by. When our values are not truly our own, our priorities become out of sync with who we are and what we want in life. We find ourselves going down a path that is not really ours.

Let's explore a discussion I had with Peter on this topic.

Me: Peter, I noted that security is ranked as your number one priority. Can you expand on that a bit?

Peter: I've always been taught not to take unnecessary chances. So I suppose that's why I put security high on my list.

Me: Can you reflect on some of the choices you made in your life that were based on this value?

Peter: I guess my choice to join a well-established corporate company and stay there for as long as I did is one of the choices I can think of . . . *but* I don't feel happy in my current role. [*Silence*] Now that I think of it . . . maybe security isn't my value, but my dad's value. He was born during World War II, and when he was growing up, security was the most important thing. I guess I picked that up from him. Maybe it's time I reflect on my values and determine whether I'm actually living my own values or someone else's!

The good news about values is that regardless of how they formed, you can always change them. It's not an easy task, but when you're aware of how your values are affecting your choices, it helps you determine if they are serving you well. In Peter's case, they clearly were not.

In order to find your rhythm, you must be aligned with your values. Are you? Let's find out with the following important exercise.

EXERCISE
VALUES ASSESSMENT

So how do you determine your core values? There are many exercises, online tools, and apps that can help you identify your top five to ten. Or you can download and print the Values Assessment Worksheet at http://www.authentes.com/finding-your-rhythm.

To get started, it's important that you set aside adequate time for this activity. Try to get relaxed. Focus your mind through meditation (go to http://www.authentes.com/finding-your-rhythm for some easy meditations, if you need guidance), and from that focused space, think about some peak experiences. Review your lifeline. Ask yourself these questions:

- *What were some of the most fantastic experiences of my life? What are the values associated with them?*
- *What were the five most terrible experiences of my life? Which values did I* not *live by when I was going through these?*

If you have a hard time creating your top-five list using these questions, download and print out the Daily Experiences Tracker Worksheet available at http://www.authentes.com/finding-your-rhythm. Every day for one week, write down what you liked and disliked the most about that day. Try to link that to values lived or not lived.

The next step is to prioritize your values. Which one is most important to you? If you have to make an important decision, which one comes first? From the values you wrote earlier, pick the top ten and list them in order of priority.

THE STORIES WE TELL OURSELVES

In this last section of Step 2, Listen to Your Rhythm, I would like to offer guidance about how to talk to yourself in a constructive way, a way that helps you get where you want to be and is aligned with your personal rhythm.

I love the Rolling Stones. I saw them play a few times in big arenas and could listen to their music every day. But there is one song I have a problem with—I'm sure you know it. Some of the words in the chorus are:

You can't always get what you want.

I really don't like that sentence. We tell ourselves all the time that we can't, we should, we must, we want, we need. And we also hear these sentiments in songs and television shows. These disempowering thoughts are everywhere, and so it's not surprising that we've incorporated them into the stories we tell ourselves and the beliefs we create for ourselves.

Words have power. They start simply, as words, but then they turn into thoughts, feelings, and emotions, and as we come to closely associate with these thoughts, they turn into beliefs. Those beliefs determine how we behave. And our behavior determines the results we get. Who says words aren't powerful?

Imagine these words spoken from a father to his son:

Words: You are never going to achieve anything in your life.

Belief: *I am no good. I will never be able to get a good job or make any money. My father will never be proud of me. No one will ever be proud of me. No one will ever love me. And I probably deserve that.*

Behavior: Playing small. Always pleasing. Always longing for external recognition.

Words create beliefs. Beliefs create behavior. And behavior creates results.

ELIMINATING *SHOULD*, *WANT*, AND *NEED*

According to the Hebrew Bible, God created the world with words. He spoke and the world came into being. The Aramaic word *abracadabra* means "I create as I speak." Aramaic is the language the Bible was written in, so this concept has been around for some time. The words you speak are the starting point for the life you generate for yourself.

Let's look at an example.

Imagine it is New Year's Eve. You are standing in a circle with your family, and you have all promised to share your intentions for the new year. You've always been intrigued by meditation. You've read about it, but you haven't yet started a practice. Everyone is sharing their intentions: "I want to get more fit." "I need to lose twenty kilograms." Now it's your turn. You give it some thought, and you say, "I really should start meditating this year."

Now how's *that* for exciting? I can't wait for the fireworks to go off! Or not? We use the word *should* all the time. *I should be more proactive in meetings, I should speak up more, I should find another job. I should, I must, I should, I must.*

Should and *must* are not words with a lot of energy. They create pressure and guilt.

Two other interesting words are *want* and *need.* If you want something, or if you need something, you create a desire. You are basically saying that you do not have something or that you lack something. A coach I worked with reminded me that the Buddha said that all desire leads to suffering. So every statement in your head where you want or need something is actually creating suffering! My sessions with that coach always included conversation along these lines:

Coach: This feeling that you are now experiencing, is that related to the need for safety, control, or approval?

Me: Safety.

Coach: Can you imagine a moment where you felt safe?

Me: Yes.

Coach: Keeping that feeling of safety in you, can you imagine letting go a little bit of the need to feel safe? And a bit more? And a bit more? And keeping that feeling of safety in you, can you imagine having safety? So, what feels better? *Having* safety, or *wanting* safety?

The sessions were always recorded, and it was incredible to see how my face changed, my posture changed, even the tone of my voice changed the moment I stopped wanting.

EXERCISE

FROM WANTING TO HAVING

So you'll feel the difference between wanting and needing to do something versus choosing to do something, I invite you to try this exercise. Think about something you would like to do as part of your daily routine—for example, yoga, meditation, or eating better. Choose something that you'll be stressed about if you don't make the time to do it. Use that word in the following exercise.

I should ________________________________ more.
(Pause and reflect on how you feel.)

I could ________________________________ more.
(Pause and reflect on how you feel.)

I can ________________________________ more.
(Pause and reflect on how you feel.)

I am excited to ________________________________ more.
(Pause and reflect on how you feel.)

I am excited to ________________________________ more

because ________ [REASON] ________ .
(Pause and reflect on how you feel.)

The next time you tell yourself you *should* do something, notice your choice of words and try to convert the *should* to a more positive and engaging statement. It will make all the difference!

USING POSITIVE LANGUAGE

Another element of language to focus on is the use of positive phrasing. You may be familiar with the example of how, if you're told, "Don't think about a pink elephant!" immediately a pink elephant will materialize in your head. Your brain doesn't pick up the word *don't*. If you say, "I don't want to be fat anymore," your brain will focus on the word *fat*. This type of self-talk does not stimulate goal achievement. Instead, say something like, "I choose to start exercising and eating nutritious food so that I will feel healthy and fit." That will get you a lot further.

Don'ts cause self-fulfilling prophecies. Imagine two race car drivers who are going three hundred kilometers an hour and plan to overtake their opponents just before the next lap. One driver tells himself, *Oh my god, I am going too fast and will definitely crash into that wall!* The other tells himself, *I can do it!* Who do you think has a higher chance of success?

So the next time you start to say, "Why not?" when invited and agreeing to do something, replace it with "Sounds good!" Or when someone asks you how you are doing, replace the "I can't complain" with "Everything is going well, thank you!" Do you feel the difference?

KEY BEATS

In this chapter we took the second step on the Finding Your Rhythm journey: Listen to Your Rhythm. We discovered that there are many ways to self-reflect and get a good understanding of your current life rhythm. Here are the main points we discussed:

- You can use the wellness wheel and psychometric analysis to create a solid overview of where you are today and your current life rhythm.
- Creating your own lifeline provides an overview of your most significant experiences, allowing you to explore and learn from the moments when you were very happy or unhappy.
- Your life did not randomly play out the way you plotted it on your lifeline. You made choices along the way. We explored the reference points you used for making these choices.
- Our beliefs and values start forming in childhood from our environment, and we carry them into adulthood. Periodically we must check to ensure that our beliefs and values are our own, and that our behaviors and decisions are aligned with reality and what matters most to us.

- The words we use have an impact on how we behave and live our lives. Our choice of words is important for how we describe our current rhythm and will also be important when we start talking about our dreams.

In the next chapter, you'll learn how to determine the life rhythm you'd like to create for yourself.

DREAM YOUR RHYTHM

You see things; and you say, "Why?" But I dream things that never were; and I say, "Why not?"
—George Bernard Shaw

Are you ready for some action? Because this is where the fun starts! In Step 3 of your Finding Your Rhythm journey, we are going to visualize a life that is fully aligned with who you really are. You will answer the question "What is the rhythm I would like to hear?"

As you go through this chapter, I invite you to open your mind. This is the dreaming phase of the program, after all, so the more you can expand your thinking of what's possible, the better. One way to do this is to approach things with what is called a **beginner's mind**.

Beginner's mind is the translation of the Japanese word *shoshin* (初心), used in Zen Buddhism. It means having an openness, an eagerness, and a lack of preconceptions when you look at something. It's akin to looking at something as if for the very first time.

Next time you eat dinner, try to approach the activity with a beginner's mind. Look at what's in front of you and approach your food as if you have no idea what to expect. Try to experience the textures and smells as if you were eating for the first time. Look at your plate. Look at your knife and fork. Look at everything as if you were a complete dinner-eating beginner. Be thankful for and appreciative of every bite. I am convinced that eating your dinner like this will completely transform your enjoyment of it!

When you were a child, you had little knowledge. You were constantly learning: how to walk, talk, listen, eat. You were curious: "Why?" "Why not?" "Is that true?" You asked your parents these questions constantly. However, as you grew older and started forming answers to these questions on your own, you asked them far less frequently. It makes sense that when you were satisfied with an answer, your curiosity was satisfied too.

With your answer in hand and your curiosity satisfied, your mind transformed that learning into truth. The other interesting thing about this process is that once you've learned something, it can be hard to accept other viewpoints.

A recent example of this dynamic in action is the public freak-out over the Covid vaccines. Remember all the stories on social media? The vaccine would cause autism. It would cause infertility. After receiving the vaccine, you needed to stay away from your children because you would be radioactive. The vaccine contained a little microchip so that the Chinese or Bill Gates (I have seen many different versions of this one) could track you through the new 5G network. And, by the way, the 5G network caused Covid in the first place. I could go on for a long time. Once stories like these are in our heads, even science has a hard time convincing us that there's no truth to any of them. When we hear something, we sometimes find it difficult to change our viewpoints about it.

The problem that arises when we stop asking questions, or when we accept as truth everything we hear, is that we stop learning. And when we stop learning, we limit the ways in which we get to know the world.

Fortunately, the antidote to learning blockages is a beginner's mind, which helps us stay open-minded and "unlearn." Retrieving your beginner's mind is a bit like meditation. Just as you can learn to observe your thoughts instead of allowing them to take over your life, returning to a beginner's mind requires learning to observe your preconceptions and judgments. A beginner's mind is free of expectation and filled with curiosity. It is uncluttered and open to every possibility. You are not applying any filters. Approaching the world with a beginner's mind doesn't mean you can't apply your critical thinking skills—it's fine to do that, but be sure you don't close off your mind to other possibilities prematurely; be critical after you have soaked up all the viewpoints and information. Don't restrict yourself. Go for it. Create your rhythm!

In the beginner's mind there are many possibilities, but in the expert mind there are few.
—Shunryū Suzuki

FINDING YOUR PURPOSE

What are you passionate about? What drives you? What is your life's purpose? Why are you here? We've all explored these questions at various points in our lives. Essentially, they're trying to get at our "why." And if we know our why, ostensibly we will have purpose in life, do meaningful work, and be happy and fulfilled, living in a way that's fully aligned with who we are. Fully in sync with our rhythm.

I too periodically struggle with these questions. Is our life's purpose something we're born with—is it in our DNA? If so, why do some of us spend our whole lives trying to figure out what it is?

I have discovered through coaching many people over the years that the struggle to find our purpose in life is a common one. Some of the drive to find answers has to do with not wanting to waste precious time on things we're not meant to do. But mostly, the push is to discover things that really give us energy, things that are fully aligned with who we are, things that are bigger than our own personal satisfaction. We want to feel that we matter in this world.

Can you recall a time when you started working on something and completely forgot about everything around you? You know, the projects that brought you into the flow and made you forget to eat, drink, and go to the bathroom? Those projects are in line with your purpose.

So how can you find or clarify that purpose? There are many articles, books, and blogs dedicated to this question. One concept that has become popular and that can help you in this work is *ikigai*, Japanese for "a reason for being."

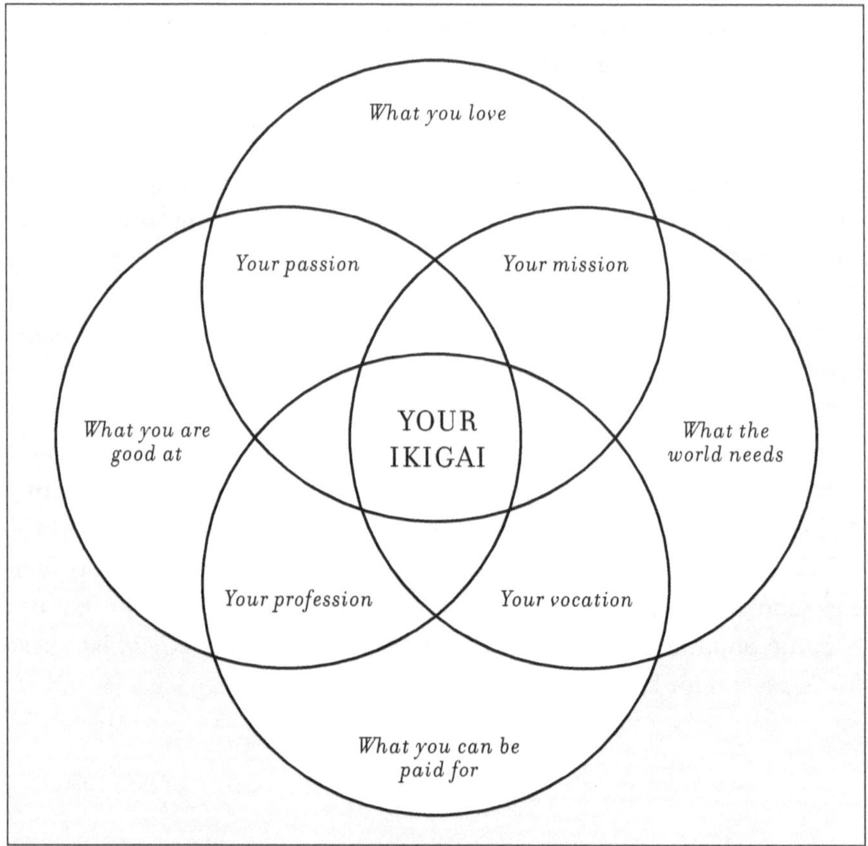

Figure 6. Your ikigai

Ikigai takes four basic elements—what you are good at, what you love, what the world needs, and what you can be paid for—and shows us that it is where those four elements intersect that we can find our purpose, our flow. In the ikigai approach, each element is just as important as the others, and if any one of them is missing in what you are currently doing, what you are doing might not be your reason for being. Let's take a closer look at the four elements.

What You Are Good at

When people think about what they're good at doing, regular job evaluations are what typically come to mind. Unfortunately, most of these evaluations assess areas of improvement rather than strengths. But identifying your strengths, your talents, and your gifts is an important step in the process of determining your ikigai.

EXERCISE
WHAT ARE MY GIFTS?

Grab your journal and write answers to the following questions:

- *What are the things I do well with little effort?*
- *In which areas do I receive positive feedback about my work?*
- *In which areas would additional training help me to become even better?*
- *What have I done to make a positive difference in the lives of others?*

If you are still struggling to come up with a list of things you're good at, ask ten people you know to give you input. Write down their answers. Review what they told you and compare this information with your own assessment.

What You Love (and What Sacrifices You Are Willing to Make along the Way)

In an article on his website, international motivational speaker Mark Manson talks about the seven strange questions that help you find your life purpose.[59] The first question he asks is "What is your favorite flavor of shit sandwich, and does it come with an olive?" Interesting question, right? What he's implying is that doing what you love doesn't come without some sacrifice. In other words, you have to know how much you're willing to struggle in order to do what you're passionate about. By the way, the word *passion* comes from the Latin verb *patior*, which means "to suffer." When we are truly passionate about something, if it is something we really *love* to do, we are willing to suffer for it.

In his book *Outliers*, Malcolm Gladwell talks about the 10,000-Hours Rule, which states that people who perform at a world-class level, such as professional musicians, artists, or athletes, have practiced for approximately ten thousand hours to get to that level of mastery.[60] This book and its conclusions received a lot of criticism that the number of hours is only part of the truth. But the point is that to become really good at something, you have to work hard to get there. If you want to be a writer, you have to spend many hours writing—and be prepared to see your work rejected many times before you become successful. If you want to be a great musician or the next Rolling Stones, go for it: put in the hard work.

Going back to Mark Manson's question, think about what *suffering* you are willing to endure, or have already endured, to become really good at something. That should give you some guidance. If you aren't willing to put in the time and effort to become good at something you thought you would love to do, you're probably on the wrong track.

EXERCISE
WHAT DO I LOVE?

To explore what you really love doing, write the answers to the following questions in your journal:

- *What would I do if I won the lottery and never had to work for money again?*
- *What do I do on weekends?*
- *What topic can I talk about for hours without getting bored?*
- *Which activity makes me forget time?*

To find more examples of what you're passionate about, you might also take a look at the lifeline you created in Step 2, or review your Daily Experiences Tracker. If you haven't yet completed that, download and print the worksheet at my website.

What the World Needs

Think of this part of ikigai as your mission statement. When you are out in the world, what are some of the things you see that you could help with? Approach it as if you were coming up with an idea for your own company. What are the unmet needs? What are your potential customers looking for?

When I started writing this book in the middle of the Covid-19 pandemic, I began thinking about how people are looking for ways to interact virtually that also bring them closer together, and how, because people had more time for self-reflection during lockdown, there seemed to be an increased need for coaching to support people in rebuilding their lives. I also noticed the need for divorce lawyers after many married couples couldn't stand the test of being in a house together for extended periods during the pandemic. I figured that I could meet those needs by producing a book that encouraged self-reflection, self-care, and strong relationships.

EXERCISE
WHAT DOES THE WORLD NEED?

Based on what is going on around you, give some thought to what unmet needs you could potentially address. Explore your answers to these questions in your journal:

- *Which problems in society would I like to help solve?*
- *What issues in the world touch me emotionally when I read about them in the news?*
- *Will these issues still be relevant in five to ten years?*

What You Can Be Paid for

We do need to make a living at the end of the day. So the question of what you can be paid for is important. But let's take this question further: Are people willing to pay for what you have to offer? Do you know if other people get paid for this? Is it your experience that people are willing to pay you for the work you love doing?

Sometimes people underestimate the value of the services they can offer. But if you know more about a certain topic than 80 percent of the population, there could be an opportunity for you to get paid for the services you can offer based on your knowledge.

EXERCISE
WHAT CAN I BE PAID FOR?

Consider these questions and write your responses in your journal:

- *Have I been paid for doing something I love?*
- *Are other people being paid for doing something I love?*
- *What skills have I developed that people are willing to pay for?*

I have noticed that many of my clients understate their capabilities and the value of their experience. They have an especially hard time identifying the things they are good at. It's hard for them to believe that they are already at a level where people would be interested in their services. For example, here's a discussion I had with one of my clients:

Bianca: I would really like to teach my own yoga classes, but I'm just a beginner. What do I know? Thinking about yoga is like thinking about the universe—it's so big. I will always need to continue to learn, and even then, I will never be able to fully understand everything there is to know about yoga.

Me: Bianca, can you talk a bit about how long you've been doing yoga and the training you've done so far?

Bianca: Unfortunately, I started very late. I wish I had started when I was young. I've probably been practicing yoga for seven or eight years. A few years ago, I did go through the two-hundred-hour yoga teacher training, and I also completed an aerial yoga teacher training. Oh, and I also did a yoga lifestyle and meditation teacher training with a teacher from India for five hundred hours.

Me: Wow. That actually sounds pretty impressive! When our coaching session is over, I cannot wait to hear more about your yoga practice. There must be a lot you can teach me!

Bianca: Mmmm . . . I guess I can. Now that I'm talking about it like this, I actually do have a lot of experience. There will always be some people who know more, but there are also many others I can share my knowledge with!

Going through all these exercises and trying to knit it all together to find your ikigai is not an easy task. Don't try to rush this. Play with the outcome. If you don't really know what your strengths are, ask people who know you. If you have difficulty getting clarity about what you love doing, go back to the lifeline exercise and try to find the moments that made you really happy. I promise you that it will be a tremendous help if you do spend the time to reflect on this. In a TED Talk called "How to Live to Be 100+," *National Geographic* reporter Dan Buettner suggested that knowing their ikigai was one of the reasons for the longevity of the people in Okinawa.

If you're still finding it hard to pinpoint your ikigai, go to http://www.authentes.com/finding-your-rhythm for an in-depth Ikigai Worksheet. Find your reason for being, and you will also find your rhythm!

VISIONING

During the Covid-19 pandemic, I was in lockdown in Bangkok. For three months I was advised not to leave my temporary rental apartment, which consisted of 540 square feet (fifty square meters) on the thirty-seventh floor. Despite the name of the apartment building, Rhythm, it was very easy to feel miserable in this situation. Especially knowing I would be stuck there for some time.

Instead of succumbing to the misery, though, I used **visioning**. I worked to envision what I wanted my life to look like after the lockdown ended. One thing that kept repeating was an image of living close to nature or the sea. Every morning before my meditation, I pictured myself sitting on the beach—breathing the fresh air, feeling the water drops from the sea landing on my body, hearing the waves. In reality, I was sitting on the balcony listening to Bangkok traffic, but the more I did this, the stronger my feeling that I was actually on the beach.

Our brain can't tell the difference between what's real and what isn't. In a study conducted in 1995, researchers from the National Institute of Neurological Disorders and Stroke, in Maryland, asked volunteers to learn a sequence of notes on a piano.[61] For five consecutive days, some of the volunteers actually played the notes on a piano, while others were asked to imagine playing the sequence. At the end of each day, the participants' brains were scanned to monitor their activity. One interesting outcome was that the brains of the people actually playing a piano and those of the people who were just imagining playing developed in exactly the same way. So, according to our brain, what we imagine happening is actually happening!

Successful people envision their future all the time. Entrepreneurs envision the day they will ring the bell to open the stock market when their company goes public. Athletes envision winning the Olympic race they are training for: they play the movie over and over again in their heads—and not just the scenes of when they are on the podium, but the scenes of getting up in the morning, mentally and physically preparing for the race, running the race, stepping over the finish line, hearing the crowd. Everything.

EXERCISE
ENVISIONING THE FUTURE

The best way to envision your future is to write it down. Grab your journal and describe how you would like your life to look a year from now. Make your notes as detailed as possible.

- What are you doing?
- Using your five senses, what are you noticing?
- Where do you live?
- Who are you with?
- How do you feel in your environment?

Once you have written your future script, replay the cinematic version on the screen in your mind. Find a quiet place where you will be undisturbed for a few minutes. Get into a comfortable position, close your eyes, and play the movie. Watch your vision unfold scene by scene.

Practice visioning daily for two weeks. Notice if any details repeat, become stronger, or change. Continue envisioning beyond the two weeks, if you enjoy it, or whenever you are struggling with your current situation.

And perhaps the funniest part of this Exercise: be sure to have a precelebration! Refer to the "Celebrating" section in Step 5 to learn how to throw yourself a party in recognition of your future self. Doing so is not just an excuse to have a glass of champagne; research suggests that positive actions like this buffer us against negative thoughts and build resilience.

Vision Board

A good way to remind yourself of your vision is to make a vision board. Creating it will help you see your goals and dreams.

The best way to make a vision board is to find pictures that symbolize the experiences, adventures, feelings, emotions, and possessions you would like to attract to your life. Next, paste these images on a large piece of poster board. Have fun with it—include pictures, words, or anything that speaks to your dreams and goals! For example, mine included a *New York Times* bestseller list that I had Photoshopped so my book appeared as number one.

This is the vision board I created some time ago:

When you've completed your vision board, hang it where you'll see it regularly. You can also take photos of it and stick copies in conspicuous places, like on the fridge or the bathroom mirror; you can even use it as your computer background.

Make it a habit to consciously look at your vision board at least once a day. Take in the different pictures. Feel how it will be to live the life you've created. If you tell your mind that this is what you want, that this is where you want to go, your mind will start working toward that goal!

Vision Quest

In some Native American cultures, males entering adulthood complete a vision quest. The process consists of being alone in nature at a sacred site for four days. In some tribes, the elders select a specific site for each young man, while in other communities the same location has been used for generations. During the course of the four days, the young man does not eat; he is just alone with nature. He prays and cries out to the spirits, imploring them to give him a vision, one that will help him find his life purpose, learn his role in the community, and discover how to best serve the people.

When I was about forty-five years old, I was on a trip that took me high up in the mountains of Tibet. I completed a vision quest with a group of like-minded people, people that were curious to learn from Tibetan spiritual practices and to learn more about themselves. The evening before our quest, we all ventured out to pick a spot where we would spend some time alone. After selecting our power spots, we came back together and performed a ritual to ask for guidance from our ancestors. We agreed to bring our notebooks and write down whatever insights or thoughts came to us and to share them with each other the following evening. We also agreed to summarize our experience in a haiku, a short form of Japanese poetry that consists of three phrases with a syllabic pattern five-seven-five. To be frank, all of this sounded like a very "mental" exercise to me, and I had some doubts about how well it would work.

When I woke up early the next morning and felt the cold mountain air on my body, I didn't know what to expect. Silently, each of us walked to the spot we had selected the day before. When I arrived at my spot, I leaned on a big rock to rest. Initially I felt calm. I looked around and started watching the clouds form different patterns. But after some time, my thoughts started to crowd in, asking what this was all supposed to mean. I thought, *This is crazy. Standing here looking at clouds and expecting to get some miraculous insight.* The mental chatter was followed by calm again.

And then I heard a strange noise. I turned to see a big yak bull coming toward me. He was moving at a pretty fast pace and making a noise that did not sound too friendly. I felt anxiety, I felt fear, and I froze. I did not think it wise to try to get away. I figured that the only option was to stay in place and send the yak as much love and empathy as I had in me—and that was what I did.

The yak's reaction was amazing: He slowed down, came to a few meters from where I was standing, and just looked at me. He then lay down on the ground in front of me in my power spot. After he had spent some time with me, the yak got up, looked at me, slowly turned around, and walked away. I had never felt as connected to nature as I did in that moment. Since we did not bring iPhones or cameras on our vision quest, I couldn't get a photo of the actual yak. But this picture should give you some indication of the sort of animal that came stomping toward me.

When we arrived back at our tents, we all spent some time working on our haiku. I thought and thought about how to fit what I wanted to say into the five-seven-five pattern, but I just couldn't get it to work—until I let go. As soon as I released my compulsive need to think my way to the best poem ever, the haiku that summarized my day came out:

> ***My connection to***
> ***The beauty that surrounds me***
> ***Will open my heart***

I have used this haiku many times since that trip. Whenever I am stuck in my thinking, this poem serves as a reminder of what's really important to me—it helps me refocus on where I get my energy from, and it reminds me how important it is that I connect to nature. I made a regular habit of leaving the city to embrace the beauty of nature.

It's amazing what one long weekend a month in nature does for me when I am normally surrounded by skyscrapers and urban busyness. If nature can recharge my battery, it can do the same for you—and make you much more productive when you return! But as you now know, if you can't get out into nature, you can still benefit from its invigorating properties by simply spending a few minutes visualizing being there.

Embodying Your Vision

In his book *At Your Command*,[62] Neville Goddard writes, "In the awareness of being all things are possible." What he means is that if you can bring something into your awareness, you can turn it into your reality. If you start acting and feeling happy, you will be happy. You can create that reality!

But he also talks about the flip side of this truth: if you tell yourself that you are unhappy, you will probably be unhappy. That's how the universe works. This concept can seem far-fetched though. How could it be possible that we create our own reality with our thoughts? What is the science behind this?

One thing quantum physics tells us is that the world is not a solid, physical place. In fact, everything we see around us, including our own body, is 99.999999999999 percent empty space. We are all made out of atoms, which are made of electrons, protons, and neutrons. Inside each atom is a central point, the nucleus. The electrons are going around the nucleus. If the nucleus were the size of a peanut, the atom would be the size of a baseball stadium! It is not too hard to imagine how much space there would be between a peanut lying in the middle of a baseball field and the outer walls of an otherwise completely empty stadium. There is actually so much empty space in an atom that if we humans were to eliminate all the space from our atoms, our whole species would fit into a sugar cube.

But if that's true—if there's so much extra *space* inside everything— why don't we just fall through our chairs? Why do we take a solid form? One way to understand this is to look at a fan: If the fan is turned off and the blades aren't moving, you can stick your hand into it. Nothing happens. But sticking your hand into a moving fan would not be a good idea. There is something in the seemingly empty space between the parts of the atom: *energy*. And if all that empty space is energy, it's an easy leap to understand that everything consists of energy. Everything is one big energy field.

Our thoughts send energy waves into this field. And guess what? If your thoughts are anxious, angry, or fearful, they radiate a certain energy wave that attracts the wave pattern you are broadcasting. So if you're thinking, *I will never be able to make my sales numbers this year*, guess what? You probably won't, because your negative thought is attracting negative energy, which has the same vibration as your negative thoughts and keeps you from mobilizing. What if, instead, you think, *I know I am capable of making my sales numbers.* Or, even better, *It feels so good to have met my target this year!* That feels different, doesn't it? The vibrations of your positive thoughts are attracting the energy that's in sync with them, and you literally feel more upbeat! This is how thoughts work, and this is why visioning, including embodying and reminding yourself of your vision, is important.

For many years, Buddhists have told us that we create our reality with our own mind. But that was always hard to prove, and we humans like to prove and understand how things work. The good news is that science, and specifically quantum physics, has made a lot of progress over the last decades. We now have scientific evidence that it's actually true: we create our reality with our own mind.[63]

So how do you embody your vision for your future self? As spiritual teacher Dr. Joe Vitale says, it's now time to "Nevillize"[64]—a term referring to self-help author Neville Goddard, used to mean bringing your vision to your conscious awareness. In other words, live your vision as if it were happening right now, or has happened already. Don't tell yourself you want or need whatever it is you have envisioned. No, you already have it!

Remember that your brain doesn't know the difference between what's real and what's imaginary. So if your vision involves you getting up in the morning and taking a walk on the beach, don't tell yourself how much you would like that—live it! Be on that beach. Feel it as if it were real. As you walk back to your envisioned home, reflect on how good that walk on the beach was, and how wonderful you felt being there. When you go over to the coffee machine and make yourself a cappuccino, smell the fresh coffee beans. Taste the coffee while you're sitting on your envisioned back porch. You are there now. Doesn't that feel fantastic?

EXERCISE
ACT LIKE THE FUTURE IS NOW

To start "Nevillizing" your vision, grab your journal and write a story about a day in the life of you, based on the life you created on your vision board. Write as if you're reflecting back on your day after you've experienced it, and make it specific. For example: *I got up this morning at 6:00 a.m. I saw the sunlight coming into my bedroom and felt the ocean breeze through the open doors. Every day I feel so grateful to wake up to the sound of the waves!* Talk about what you experienced, where you were, how you felt, who you were with. It's OK if your day doesn't address all the pictures on your vision board, because it probably wouldn't be physically possible to do everything on the board in one day. But do try to speak to the essence of your board when writing.

After you've finished your "Day in the Life of You," reread the story at least once a day. Really try to be in that life when you read it—feel as if it has already happened!

I've always disliked people telling me that it's "all in my head" when I'm unhappy about things not going as I had planned. But I guess it is! When you start directing your thoughts toward what you would like to achieve in life, the world changes. Stop wanting and start having. Even if you don't believe that the universal powers work this way, if you start embodying your vision or acting as if the future is now, you will start behaving in a way that is aligned with your vision for yourself. And that will make a difference!

> *If you don't know where you are going, you'll end up someplace else.*
>
> —Yogi Berra

KEY BEATS

In this chapter we took the third step of the Finding Your Rhythm journey: Dream Your Rhythm. We explored how to find your purpose, so you can be the person you want to be. We also looked at how you can envision and then start attracting your dream life.

We discussed several key points:

- Having a beginner's mind is important to ensure you remain open to the opportunities in front of you.
- Ikigai, or your "reason for being," encompasses what you're good at, what you love, what the world needs, and what you can be paid for.
- Your purpose can guide you in all decision-making.
- You can make your dreams tangible by envisioning the life you wish for yourself through

  - visioning,
  - creating a vision board, and
  - going on a vision quest.

Now that you've developed a clear picture of your dream life, the next chapter will help you change your life, taking you from where you are today to where you want to be. Buckle up!

TURN THE BEAT AROUND

True life is lived when tiny changes occur.
—Leo Tolstoy

Do you remember the movie *Groundhog Day*, with Bill Murray and Andie MacDowell? If you haven't seen it, the movie is about a cynical TV reporter who is covering an annual Groundhog Day event in a small town in the US. This reporter gets trapped in a time loop that forces him to repeat the same day over and over again. I won't spoil the rest of the movie for you, but I bring it up to illustrate the following point: it's hard to change. We created beliefs for ourselves that resulted in habits we've picked up along the way. Those habits are the way we behave. And if we do not change our beliefs and our habits, our life will continuously repeat itself. Just like it did in *Groundhog Day*.

Fortunately, we can do something about that. By becoming more aware of our repetitive negative thoughts, we can change our automatic responses to those thoughts—our automatic behaviors—so our actions are more in line with where we want to go. When we change our automatic behaviors, we are essentially getting rid of habits that no longer serve us.

Change is hard—but to get your dream life, it's worth it. And it can be done!

Habits

We all have habits—some that are good for us, and some that are not so good or even bad for us. The problem is that you can't just eliminate a bad habit. In order to make a lasting change, the bad habit needs to be replaced with a good habit that can serve as a substitute. As Charles Duhigg describes in his book *The Power of Habit*,[65] a habit consists of three elements:

1. cue
2. behavior
3. reward

The **cue** is the trigger for the habit, the **behavior** is the action that follows, and the **reward** is whatever craving is satisfied by the action. Let me give you an example. In one of the common areas of my former workplace, there was always a big plate piled with candy and sweets. You couldn't miss it if you walked past. Over time, I began eating a lot of these candies during the day, and I was doing it without thinking. But when I started paying attention to my new habit, I discovered that the trigger for my candy craving was finishing a work task. Every time I completed something (a call, reviewing a report, a meeting) I would walk over to grab a candy. The act of finishing a task was the cue, and walking to the common area to get candy was the behavior.

Interestingly, I was having a hard time discerning the reward. Most people would assume that the reward was the candy. But I didn't really *need* the candy. There was something else I needed that I couldn't quite put my finger on . . . What was the craving I was trying to satisfy? Was I needing the exercise of walking? Eventually it dawned on me that my craving was to feel free. As I mentioned earlier, freedom is a big driver for me, and being stuck in an office, even though it was a corner office with a beautiful view, did not make me feel very free. Stepping outside my office was satisfying my need for freedom.

After I figured out what the true need was, I started playing around with different behaviors. I tried going for short walks. I looked out the window more often. Over time, I found that there were other behaviors that could satisfy my need to feel free. By implementing a new habitual behavior, I was able to stop eating the office candy.

In order to change our habits, we first must become more aware of them. Even though habits make up 40 to 45 percent of our daily lives,[66] we hardly notice that our behavior is based on very predictable patterns.

If you start reviewing or paying attention to your habits, you'll see that you have hundreds of them. I initially struggled to notice mine because they are stored so deep in my unconscious mind!

To increase my awareness, I started carrying a small notepad and writing down the things I did while on autopilot. I realized there were a lot of things I was doing without thinking about them: Picking up my phone when I woke up to turn off the alarm and taking a sneak peek at my email. Running the same route around the lake every day. Grabbing a snack from the kitchen when I got home, even if I wasn't hungry. Getting up and doing something else when I got stuck while writing. The list went on and on.

I also noticed that I had supportive and unsupportive habits. Supportive habits help us realize our vision. Unsupportive habits block us from realizing our vision or slow down the process. Sometimes it's hard to tell which is which! For example, walking away when I am stuck with writing could be a good habit if I use the time to clear my head and find inspiration. If I just walk away to start doing something else as an escape, it could be a serious roadblock to finishing what I started.

Another interesting thing about habits is that a few key ones seem to trigger or override others. For example, when I started running every day to prepare myself for my first half marathon, it triggered a number of other habits. I used to have wine with my dinner every day and sometimes another glass later in the evening. But when I started running, I stopped doing that. I also stopped eating those tasty-looking granola bars from the coffee shop, and I went from two or three cappuccinos per day to one. I also started stretching every day to prepare my muscles for the longer runs. The key habit of running triggered a lot of other good habits and motivated me to replace some bad ones.

Unfortunately this can also go the other way. Say, for example, that you stopped smoking a year ago, but recently developed the habit of having *just one* cigarette in the morning. It's easy to see how that habit could easily lead to smoking more—*One more won't hurt!*—and then, when exercising becomes more difficult because of the habit, decreasing your exercise levels.

Remember how we spoke about "chunking" in the first chapter, and how it can help you form a new, supportive habit? Pairing a new task with something you already do will significantly increase your chances of making the new habit stick!

It's important to start paying attention to your habits, because once you do, you'll notice how many you do unconsciously—and how many are not constructive to the rhythm you would like to create for yourself.

Again I encourage meditation, yoga, and spending time in nature in order to cultivate the awareness critical to recognizing your habits. Then you can embrace the supportive ones and replace the unsupportive ones. Also, your daily journal should give you a lot of insight into the habits that you have developed.

To further help you identify your habits and better understand why you fall back into certain ones, try the next exercise. You can use your journal or download and print out a helpful worksheet at http://www.authentes.com/finding-your-rhythm.

EXERCISE
TRACKING MY HABITS

Spend some time over the next few days tracking the things you do on autopilot, as well as any habits you do deliberately. Your list might be long, and that's OK. The idea is to make note of all your habits in order to increase your awareness of them. Remember, a habit consists of three elements: cue, behavior, reward.

After you've tracked your habits for several days, review your list. Then choose a few that you want to explore further. Perhaps you want to know why you do a particular behavior. Or maybe there's a specific behavior you've been wanting to change. For each of the identified habits, answer the following prompts in your journal or on the worksheet.

The habit I would like to explore:	
What is the cue?	*What is the reward?*
For four to five days, keep track of the following when you recognize the urge to follow this habit: • Where am I? ________________ • What time is it? ______________ • Who else is around? ___________ • What did I just do? ___________ • What is my emotion? _________	Reflecting on the cues, fill in your thoughts about what craving the habit satisfies: Reward theory: ___________________ How do I feel? ___________________ Is the craving gone? Y/N If you circled *Y*, you have found the reward for your habit. If *N*, give some more thought to what the craving is that wants to be satisfied. Consider repeating this process until you've found a clear answer.

Once you've identified the reward for a specific habit, you can start thinking about how you can change your behavior when you get the urge to follow the habit. In other words, when the cue is there, how can you satisfy your need for that reward in a healthier way?

WHY PEOPLE DON'T LIKE CHANGE

A few years ago, I was coaching two managers from the same company. Both Linda and Mark had been with the company for more than ten years and had worked hard to make their way up the corporate ladder to management positions. One beautiful spring morning, they were asked to join the company's top fifty managers for an important surprise meeting. Linda and Mark were proud to be part of that group, and they were excited and a little nervous when the CEO and the full executive team walked into the room.

The CEO walked up to the microphone and announced, "Ladies and gentlemen, fellow colleagues, I have great news to share. As some of you already know, later today we will announce the merger between our company and XYZ Corporation. With this merger we will become the biggest powerhouse in the telecommunications industry. I couldn't be prouder of what we have achieved! We'll provide more details in a meeting next week, but we wanted all of you to know before we tell the media today around noon. Until that time, please don't discuss this with anyone outside the group in this room. Congratulations. We have an exciting future ahead of us!"

Linda called me later that day and said, "Karel, do you have time for a coaching session tomorrow? You've probably seen the exciting news that we are merging with XYZ Corporation. As you can imagine, there will be a lot of changes, and I would like to have a discussion with you about the opportunities that will arise from this merger and how I can best prepare myself. The merger will probably result in many organizational changes; new positions will be created, and some positions will no longer be needed. This feels like an excellent time to think about how I can advance my career!"

Of course I had time for Linda, and the next day we had a great session, during which she created her plan and her vision for her role with the company going forward.

The call from Mark was somewhat different. "Karel, do you have time for a coaching session tomorrow? You've probably seen the news that we are merging with XYZ Corporation. As you can imagine, there will be a lot of changes and I am very afraid of what will happen. I haven't been in my role for too long, and there's a risk that my position will not be needed anymore—or that I'll be replaced by someone from XYZ because my area is one of their biggest strengths. I would like to talk to you about how I can prepare a plan to limit my risks and maybe start looking at other career opportunities. The CEO mentioned this morning that some managers were already aware of this merger; I was not, so that's probably not a good sign. Karel, I'm not happy about this. I could really use your help."

I also met with Mark the next day, and we managed to turn his thinking around to a more positive direction. But can you see the difference in how these two people responded to exactly the same news? The facts were the same. They had both heard the CEO tell the same story. But they interpreted the message in two totally different ways.

When we hear about upcoming changes, we interpret the information based on what's stored in our unconscious minds. And if we are not aware that this is happening, we can develop all kinds of negative thoughts, followed by physical reactions—fear, anxiety, stress. And the corresponding behavior will follow.

We like to stay in our comfort zones. In the example above, Mark had a hard time pushing himself to explore new opportunities. He was stuck in what was familiar—his current position, which felt comfortable and safe. His fear of the unknown was keeping him there.

In a classic psychology experiment by Robert M. Yerkes and John D. Dodson,[67] the researchers concluded that people need a certain level of stress to perform at a steady level—but only up to a certain point. When the stress increases beyond that point due to unpredictability, uncontrollability, or other threats, performance decreases. Other research suggests that when confronted with the choice between a situation with a known risk or one with an unknown risk, most people will go for the comfortable, known-risk option, even if there is a likelihood that the riskier choice potentially could have a better outcome.[68]

So for optimal performance, you need a certain level of anxiety. If you always work from what you know, life can become repetitive and dull. Although people generally dislike leaving their comfort zones, this uncomfortable zone is where the magic happens, where learning starts. However, if you take it too far and the anxiety becomes too overwhelming, there's an opposite effect: your productivity will go down. The optimal state is the one where you feel challenged but not overstretched.

So what's holding us back from change? Even in situations where we know that change will be good for us, we sometimes just can't make it happen. We know that we should be eating healthier food and skipping those unhealthy snacks during the day, but we struggle to follow through. At our New Year's Eve party, we promise ourselves and everyone with us that we will start exercising. But even when our annual physical indicates that our fitness level is very low and our blood pressure is too high, we still struggle to follow through. Fitness clubs make a lot of money from annual memberships initiated in January; a significant number of people show up for about two months and merely hope to go for another ten . . . Why?

Five Inner Hindrances

One of the reasons we falter in reaching our goals lies in the difficulty of making lasting change. As we discussed earlier, making change is hard because we have repetitive negative thoughts that lead to automatic negative behaviors, which form unsupportive habits.

But there's another school of thought that helps explain the challenge in making change. In a TEDx Talk, Shaolin master Shi Heng Yi spoke about the five inner hindrances that prevent us from reaching our goals.[69] In the Buddhist tradition, these hindrances are identified as mental factors that can "color" your mind, much like pictures projected onto a movie screen. We often focus on the pictures being projected onto the screen and do not notice the screen itself. These mental factors can hinder our progress in meditation and in our daily lives.

The five hindrances are

1. sensory desire (*kāmacchanda*)
2. ill will (*vyāpāda*; also spelled *byāpāda*)
3. sloth and torpor (*thīna-middha*)
4. restlessness and worry (*uddhacca-kukkucca*)
5. doubt (*vicikicchā*)

SENSORY DESIRE

The first hindrance to making change has to do with seeking happiness through the five senses of sight, sound, smell, taste, and physical feeling. To explain this, let's imagine that you recently went to the doctor for an annual checkup and discovered that you're overweight and have hypertension. You decide to decrease your stress and increase your fitness by trying a twelve-week program that will help you train for a 3K run. You buy the shoes, the Garmin watch, the subscription to the exercise tracker app. You are ready to go!

On the morning of your very first training day, you wake up and start putting on your fitness gear . . . and then you smell the bacon and eggs that your partner is preparing for the rest of the family. You love that smell! You think, *I can't miss that delicious breakfast!* So you decide to postpone the first running day to Monday. *Monday is a better day to start this anyway,* you tell yourself. But on Monday your partner starts cuddling with you when you wake up, and you love that touch so much you decide to postpone your training to another day. This is how the sensory desire hindrance affects you.

ILL WILL

Ill will refers to thoughts of rejection toward something, along with feelings of hostility, resentment, hatred, or bitterness. In the Vipassana meditation tradition, ill will is referred to as *aversion.* When you have an aversion to something, you do not like it, do not want to do it, and try to avoid it.

Ill will is the opposite of the sensory desire hindrance, which attracts you to something you like and compels you to cling to it. Aversion blocks us from change; we avoid doing what's best for us. For example, you might realize that you are stuck in a toxic relationship, and you know you need to make a change, but your aversion to being alone is so great that you stay where you are. Or maybe you don't like your job, but because you're averse to financial insecurity, you stay put. Once again, awareness is the key to opening the door to change. The only way to get free from the ill will hindrance is to become aware of your aversions and how they translate into your current beliefs and values.

SLOTH AND TORPOR

This hindrance to change manifests as a heaviness of body and a dullness of mind, which together can drag you down into disabling inertia and thick depression. It's also referred to as a state of being trapped—trapped without energy, you feel uninspired, bored, and sometimes even overwhelmed. This often happens after we go through a phase of not reacting to sensual desires and letting go of aversions. Having grown accustomed to the stimulation of these desires and aversions, the mind sometimes goes into a state of ennui, indifference, and defeat when these stimuli are absent. *Why am I here, anyway?* the mind will ask. *Everything seems irrelevant.* When people experience this phenomenon, they have no energy for anything. It does not mean the energy is not there; it means they have a hard time accessing the energy sources.

The antidote to sloth and torpor is self-reflection. Think about why you are here. What is it that you would like to do? Just as we discussed in Step 3, Dream Your Rhythm, ask yourself, *What is my purpose?*

Let me share an example of a coaching discussion I had with one of my clients. Christina was stuck. She'd recently retired from her role as a CEO, and without the constant stimuli that she was used to, she became bored, indifferent, and unable to decide on what she actually wanted to do.

Christina: I don't know what to do anymore, Karel. I wake up tired every morning. I have no energy to do anything!

Me: Can you tell me a bit more?

Christina: I used to have so much energy. When I was still the CEO of Brandspace Agency, I loved going to work. I loved being among all the creative people on my team. I loved everything that came with the job. The status, the great clients I worked with, the nice paycheck. But ever since the company was sold and I was let go, I just haven't been able to do anything. At first I missed everything I was used to. I kept replaying the great times I had with the team and wondering why I couldn't have that anymore. The next phase was anger. I became angry with the new owner. With myself. With everything. It felt terrible. Through your coaching I was able to let that all go. I actively used a lot of the releasing techniques you introduced me to. But now I feel like a noodle . . . not sure how to get out of this.

Me: What I am hearing, Christina, is that you have done an amazing job in letting go of craving and aversion. You let go of wanting to be in the position you were in before, the position you really liked. You also let go of the anger that came after that, the aversion to the uncertainty. You should be extremely proud of yourself. The state you are in now is very natural. Without a clear sense of purpose and meaning, this is exactly how people start to feel. Like a noodle! Let's talk about how we can get you un-noodled! What are some of the things you can do to start losing this feeling?

Christina: I guess, listening to you, I should start being more loving to myself. And embrace where I am today. And start dreaming. Start dreaming about what the future could look like. What do I need? What do I want? With that clarity, I should be able to, as you say, un-noodle myself! Can you help me with that?

When you experience mild sloth and torpor, it's time for deep inner reflection or conversations with people who can help you find your energy sources again. This could be a coach or just someone you know who is passionate about what they do and who inspires you to start developing and acting on your own purpose.

RESTLESSNESS AND WORRY

The fourth hindrance is restlessness and worry, which typically results from an inability to calm the mind. Remember the monkey mind from Step 1? No matter how hard you try to calm your monkey mind, your thoughts swing from branch to branch as you worry about what will happen in the future or what happened in the past: *I wish I could ride my motorcycle around the world. There are so many examples of people who are doing this on YouTube. But I can't. What if I get sick? What if I can't find a job after I finish the journey?* or *That was a good dinner. I really hope they liked me. What if they didn't?* This worrying doesn't get us anywhere. As long as we're worrying about the past or future, we're not living in the now—we're not fully present today.

The now, today, is all we have! It's the only thing we can change. We can't go back to the past; that is done. And we can't jump to the future because it's not there yet.

DOUBT

If we lack conviction or trust, we have doubt. In Tibetan and Indian Buddhism, doubt is mostly considered negative, a hindrance to desired change. *I doubt I will ever have the guts to quit my job* is a thought that will keep you doing what you're doing, even if you don't like it. *I doubt I will have the discipline to go to the gym three or four times a week* is a thought that will not help you realize your New Year's resolution to get fit!

But Zen philosophy takes a more positive view of doubt: the seventeenth-century Zen master Takayuki said:

> You must doubt deeply, again and again, asking yourself what the subject of hearing could be. Pay no attention to the various illusory thoughts and ideas that might occur in you. Only doubt and more deeply, gathering together in yourself all the strength that is in you, without aiming at anything or expecting anything in advance, without intending to be enlightened, and without even intending not to be enlightened; become like a child within your own breast.

The wisdom here is to avoid believing something just because someone tells you it is true. Explore ideas yourself, and then consciously decide whether you want to make certain beliefs your own.

At the end of this chapter you will develop a plan for change. For now, though, go back over the list of the five hindrances and notice whether any of them apply to situations in your life. Do you have attitudes that are keeping you from following through on goals? If so, how might you think differently? Are specific tasks, objects, or people distracting you? If so, how can you stay more focused? Are you uninspired? If so, what would make your environment more inspiring?

Change is tough, and most people naturally try to avoid it. So how do you prepare yourself for change?

GETTING READY FOR CHANGE

I have worked with many people who knew that they had to change but couldn't get themselves to do it. They'd get sidetracked by the five hindrances we just explored. I had a client who was overweight and a smoker. He knew that his lifestyle was not good for his health, but unfortunately, it took him having a heart attack to really start making lifestyle changes. Does that mean we all need something terrible to happen to us before we will consider making necessary changes? Fortunately, the answer to this question is no.

Change does not come easily. The most critical element of change is *the need for it*. But if you aren't aware that something needs to change, or your unconscious habits and beliefs are keeping you from change, nothing will happen. When you become aware of the need to change, that's when change can start.

In some cases, you'll be forced to change. As with my client who had a heart attack, you may suddenly find yourself with change thrust upon you: you might lose your job, get into a serious accident, or experience another impactful or stressful situation. But don't wait for that to happen!

If you are currently living a life that is not meant for you, if you are living someone else's life, you will start experiencing the impact at some point. The longer you wait, the more likely it is that change will be forced upon you. You may get ill, have frequent medical issues, or start feeling tired, or depressed. Let's not go there. The fact that you picked up this book and made it this far suggests that you are aware that something needs to change.

YOUR LOYAL SOLDIER

Thinking about our reluctance to change always reminds me of the story of the loyal Japanese soldier Hiroo Onoda. Mr. Onoda was the Imperial Japanese Army officer in World War II who remained on a jungle post on an island in the Philippines for twenty-nine years, refusing to believe that the war was over. He had found pamphlets saying that the war had ended, but he thought they were enemy propaganda. He, together with three other men, built bamboo huts and survived on very limited resources because they did not want to surrender.

A lot of us have our own loyal soldiers. Bill Plotkin, a psychologist and wilderness guide, describes this part of us as follows: "The Loyal Soldier [is a bold, discerning, and headstrong] sub-personality that formed during our childhood [to aid us in surviving the dysfunctional] realities of our families and culture."[70] Plotkin goes on to explain how the loyal soldier protects us through minimizing or increasing our trauma.

Think of the old you as the loyal soldier, your old beliefs and values that have brought you to where you are today. The loyal soldier's services are very much appreciated. Celebrate the old you: give that version of yourself a medal and thank that person for all the hard work and loyalty. But it is now time to tell the old you that the war is over; it's time to retire. It is time for a new you to effect change!

THE CHANGE PLAN

The time has come to bring together the lessons you've learned in Steps 1 through 4, and to continue making tangible progress on your journey to finding your rhythm. In your change plan, you'll set realistic time frames and get clarity on how to create change step by step. To get started, you will need your journal, or you can download and print out the Change Plan Worksheet from http://www.authentes.com /finding-your-rhythm.

1. Review Your Vision

Begin your change plan by looking over your vision board. (If you haven't yet created one, refer to Step 3: Dream Your Rhythm for detailed instructions.) Based on what's represented on your vision board, write up to ten personal statements about the future as if they were happening now. Here are some examples:

- I am a bestselling author.
- I have a very active social life.
- I travel three months out of each year.

2. Determine Your Desired Wellness Scores

On a new page in your journal, create a chart consisting of four columns and eight rows. (Or refer to the online worksheet at http://www .authentes.com/finding-your-rhythm). Now go back to the wellness wheel you created in Step 2: Listen to Your Rhythm. (If you haven't done this yet, there is no time like the present!) In the first column of your chart, write down each of the eight dimensions from the wellness wheel. In the second column, copy the scores you gave yourself in each dimension. In the third column, write down the scores you'd like to have based on the vision you created for yourself. Finally, in the last column, write down your gap score, or the difference between your desired score and your current score. For example, if you scored eight on financial and two on social and you would like to increase social to eight, this is what that part of the chart would look like:

Category	Current score	Desired score	Gap
Financial	8	8	—
Social	2	8	6

As you will see in the next step of this change plan, you'll use the size of the gap to prioritize your focus areas.

3. List the Changes You Would Like to Make

Based on your vision board and your gap scores, create a list of the changes you would like to make. You can do this by writing a statement about what you will have achieved when you realize each desired score.

Here are some examples of statements for each category:

1. Social: I have many friends and a very active social life.
2. Emotional: My meditation practice is supporting my emotional well-being.
3. Intellectual: I have continued my Spanish lessons.
4. Physical: I feel healthy and strong.
5. Spiritual: I have continued my regular meditation practice.
6. Occupational: I am a bestselling author.
7. Financial: I have enough money in my bank account to support a comfortable lifestyle.
8. Environmental: I have moved to an environment where I'm surrounded by creativity.

EXERCISE
DEVELOP YOUR CHANGE PLAN

On a new page in your journal, create three more columns to match the sample shown. Or refer to the online worksheet at http://www.authentes.com/finding-your-rhythm. For each category in the wellness wheel, write down your gap score and the change you would like to see. As we discussed, it can be helpful to answer the question "To reach my desired score, what do I need to achieve?" when deciding what to list in the third column. Don't worry about the action steps yet—that's something we will look at in the next step of the process.

Category	Gap Desired Score minus current score	Change To reach my desired score, I have to achieve the following:
Example: Social	6	I have a large social network. I meet with my friends regularly.
Social		
Emotional		
Intellectual		
Physical		
Spiritual		
Occupational		
Financial		
Environmental		

The dimensions with the biggest gap will have the biggest impact on your life if you commit to changing them. For the action planning that we will do in the next chapter, it's important to prioritize the dimensions. Let's focus on the areas with the biggest impact first!

Developing a change plan is not an easy task. Sometimes we get stuck in our own heads. Remember the limiting beliefs we reviewed in the "Listen to Your Rhythm" section? For example, you might believe that you can't make money doing the work you love. And that belief might convince you to change your current score for occupational well-being from a three to a seven. *My job is not that bad after all,* you might think. *And it pays good money, doesn't it?*

To avoid falling back on your limiting beliefs and old stories, I strongly suggest you find support. Why? Because as we discussed before, change is hard. It requires you to do things differently than you have done them before, and that's hard for us human beings. Your support person could be your spouse or a friend—someone who's not afraid to call you out when you fall back on old behaviors. This will put some pressure on your relationship, though, so make sure you choose your support person accordingly.

Another option, which sidesteps the personal relationship issue, is to find a professional coach who can help you stay on track. I have also seen people set up their own "board of directors." With this method, you would ask four to six friends, colleagues, or other people who will keep you honest to serve as your "board"; you meet with them first to discuss your change plan, and then on a regular basis to discuss your progress and hear their perspectives.

KEY BEATS

In this chapter we took the fourth step of the Finding Your Rhythm journey: Turn the Beat Around. We looked at how habits are formed and why they're so difficult to change. Yet, change is necessary if we are to ever find our true rhythm.

We discussed some key points:

- Change is achievable when it's broken down into small steps! As the Chinese proverb says, "A journey of a thousand miles begins with a single step."
- Our habits will keep us repeating automatic negative behaviors over and over unless we consciously decide to make a change.
- There are five hindrances that mentally prevent us from making changes: sensory desire, ill will, sloth and torpor, restlessness and worry, and doubt.
- Creating a change plan sets you up for success.

It is now time to convert your plan into action; you'll do just that in the next step: Play!

PLAY!

A goal without a plan is just a wish.
—Antoine de Saint-Exupéry

And now let's get ready for the hardest part: converting your vision, goals, and dreams into concrete action steps. You'll be working off your change plan to create your action plan, which will include information about what you are going to do and when. It will not be easy, but it's a rewarding part of the Finding Your Rhythm journey. The lessons in this chapter will allow you to start seeing your vision come to life!

We'll begin Step 5 with a review of your beliefs and values. Why? Because while your limiting beliefs are among the biggest hurdles to making lasting change—and finding your rhythm—your values are the antidote to your limiting beliefs. You will assess whether you need to work on your beliefs and values in order to realize your vision.

Then you will be guided through preparing a detailed action plan, starting with the short-term changes you wrote on your change plan.

The last step before we come to the end of this journey is to *celebrate*. Celebration creates momentum. It is a step we often forget, but one that can give us the energy we need to find our rhythm!

UPGRADING YOUR BELIEFS

Periodically your computer or phone will alert you that you need to update the operating system. The latest version will have new features that have been added in response to changing circumstances. Maybe the update is needed because of new security threats or because of a new way you're interacting with your device.

What about our own personal operating system? How often do we update it to react to changes in our environment and in our lives?

The limiting beliefs you identified in Step 2 are the first things to update. These are holding you back from realizing the vision you created in Step 3. But before we work on these, you might be wondering, *How do I change my beliefs?* That's a fair question, because while it is relatively easy to identify your limiting beliefs, changing or replacing them is hard work! Beliefs are sticky. They're embedded in your brain at an early age—so deeply embedded that you can't change them just by thinking that everything should be different.

So how do we change our beliefs? One thing we do know is that a major life experience can change our beliefs. It can change how we look at life. What can we learn from that? Let's explore.

I was working with a client named David. He was COO of a technology company and really did not like his job. We spent many coaching sessions trying to unravel the beliefs that were keeping him from changing jobs. We were making some progress, but he was struggling to execute the changes he wanted to make—until the day a doctor told him that he had cancer and only nine to twelve months to live. At that moment, all the beliefs that were holding him back disappeared. He quit his job the next day, and together with his wife spent the following year traveling to all the places they had always dreamed about. David had an amazing time, and through all this positive energy he was able to extend his time on this planet six months longer than the doctor had projected.

I almost always ask my clients the following question: "What would you do if you only had one more year to live?" Often the answer I hear is "Quit my job, or at least work a lot less. Spend more time with my family, reach out to old friends, travel the world and be happy!"

Many of the answers I get in response to my question are aligned with the findings of Bronnie Ware, an Australian palliative-care nurse who tends to patients in their last three to twelve weeks. In her book *The Top Five Regrets of the Dying*,[71] she relays the most popular regrets:

- A desire to have a life "true to myself" instead of living for others.
- A desire to have worked less.
- A desire to truly speak my feelings.
- A desire for long-lasting friendships.
- A desire to "let myself be happier."

Most of us do know what we want: people are pretty clear about it when they answer the "one year to live" question during coaching, and they are also very clear about it just before they die. This shows how difficult it is to change our programming. Someone needs to bang the drum to wake us up!

So what can we learn from this? One thing we can learn is that not everything we believe is true. When confronted with a major life experience, we suddenly realize that working too hard just to have that extra money in our bank account is not really going to make us happy. Our belief that we need another x-amount of money to be happy does turn out to be false.

What beliefs are you carrying that are completely unsupportive? Go back to the beginner's mind that we discussed earlier. What do you need to believe to live the life you want to live?

What we learned after the age of seven came mostly through repetition; we learned and then practiced, practiced, practiced. When you learned to play a musical instrument, you picked up the instrument every day for a period of time. When you learned to ride a bike, you kept at it until being on two wheels felt like second nature. Whatever you were trying to learn, you repeated the actions over and over until your subconscious mind stored them.

But some of what you have stored in your subconscious mind no longer supports you. This is where your positive beliefs come in: once you identify the beliefs you would like to embrace to realize your vision, start repeating them to yourself over and over. Put them on a sticky note on the bathroom mirror. Make them your home screen on your smart phone. Through repetition, you learn to embrace certain beliefs and store new ones in your subconscious mind. Repeat these positive beliefs until your mind absorbs them. Fake it till you make it!

Identifying and changing or replacing your limiting beliefs is hard work, but it's necessary if you want to live your life in a different rhythm! Now it's your turn to analyze your thoughts, let go of limiting beliefs, and create supporting ones.

EXERCISE
UPDATE YOUR BELIEFS

Pull out your journal or download and print the Update Your Beliefs Worksheet at http://www.authentes.com/finding-your-rhythm. Then refer to the My Limiting Beliefs exercise from Step 2 and review the five to ten beliefs you wrote down. These are the ones holding you back from realizing your vision and finding your rhythm.

Turn to a blank page and create two columns (or use the worksheet). In the first column, list the limiting beliefs you identified earlier. In the second column, indicate whether each belief is a serious impediment at this point. You may find that some beliefs really are preventing you from realizing your vision, while others are limiting but not crippling. I want you to identify the beliefs that are so strong and stubborn that, if you cannot change them, you will never realize your vision. For example, if you believe that you will never make money in a job other than your current one, it will be impossible for you to move toward the job you created for yourself in your vision; your limiting belief will always hold you back.

Now consider the beliefs that you would like to embrace—
the supporting beliefs that will help you reach a certain goal
or realize your vision. Often, a new belief is the opposite of an
old, limiting belief (*I will never make enough money doing what
I love* becomes *Doing what I love will give me the resources to
support myself and my family*), but the belief could also be a
completely new one based on the vision that you have created.
In your journal or on the worksheet, write down ten new supporting beliefs.

If, after completing this exercise, you are still struggling to identify
your limiting beliefs and develop supportive ones, you may need additional encouragement. One option is to find a coach. Breaking through
your mind chatter on your own, without a pro helping you in the process, can be really hard and frustrating.

Another suggestion is to review the validity of your beliefs using a
method developed by Byron Katie,[72] an American speaker and author
and the founder of the method of self-inquiry known as The Work. She
developed the method to break down negative thoughts and limiting
beliefs.

The four questions she uses in her method are as follows:

Question 1: Is it true? The answer to this question should be either yes
or no. If yes, go to Question 2. If no, proceed to Question 3.

Question 2: Can you absolutely know it is true? Can you prove it? Are
there hard facts that support your belief?

Question 3: How do you react when you believe that thought? Think
about a moment when you were behaving according to your belief.
How did you feel? How did you make others feel? How did you
treat yourself?

Question 4: What would you be without the thought? Let your mind
run free here. Close your eyes and observe the pictures that come
up. Experience what you would be without your belief.

Let's give it a try with an example. Suppose your limiting belief is that you can't make money doing what you love. Here we go:

Is it true? *Yes.*

Can you absolutely know it is true? *Mmmm . . . I guess not. I never really tried doing what I love. I've always just stayed in my job because I was scared that I couldn't support my family if I left.*

How do you react when you believe that thought? *I don't move. I stay where I am and accept feeling stuck and miserable. I accept the feeling to satisfy my need for security.*

Who would you be without that thought? *I would be traveling the world as a photographer and writer! It would feel so amazing! I would be doing everything I love all the time. I could do that forever!*

On http://www.authentes.com/finding-your-rhythm, I have included a link to Byron Katie's website. I invite you to take a look at some of the sessions there. It is really amazing to see how questioning the validity of our beliefs causes them to lose their power.

REVIEWING YOUR VALUES

Now that you've reviewed your beliefs, let's also take a look at how your values are hindering or supporting your vision. In his book *Awaken the Giant Within*, Tony Robbins talks about this. He writes about the differences between teaching people about discovering their own values and directing people to "consciously select or redirect the order and content of their values hierarchy system." He uses the example of switching someone's number one priority from security to adventure and demonstrates what kind of change that would play in that person's life.[73]

I think it's fair to say that any time we reorder or re-rank priorities—whether they are tasks on our to-do list or how to spend a $500 bonus—we set in motion a ripple of changes. So it's easy to see that if we were to review and reorder something as soul defining as our values, it could have a major impact on reaching (or not reaching) our vision.

Your values create the decision tree that you will use when executing your plan. Let me give you an example. One of my clients was asked to lead a group of companies in Southeast Asia; they were part of a large, multinational food company. When I met him, he explained that he was really eager to take on that role but was reluctant to work with the global company. He was afraid he would not be able to be himself. One of his main values was directness, and he feared that he could not really honor that value in this environment. When we further explored this value, he came to the conclusion that he wanted to replace it with a new one: authenticity. It was not really "being direct" he was after; it was much more about being able to share his authentic opinions. And with authenticity as a value, he could work toward sharing his opinions in a way that would fit with the environment he was in.

If he had kept directness as his number one value, he probably would have declined the role. With his new insight, however, he agreed to take the role and since then has been leading the regional group very successfully!

EXERCISE
VALUE PRIORITIZATION

In your journal, draw four columns and label them as shown (Current Values / Vision Aligned / New Values / Prioritized Values). Alternatively, print the Review Your Values Worksheet available at http://www.authentes.com/finding-your-rhythm. In the first column, list your top five to ten values as noted on the Values Assessment you completed in Step 2. In the second column, indicate yes or no pertaining to whether these values are aligned with your vision. In the third column, include the values that you have identified and would like to include but that are not on your initial list. And now the hard part: in the final column, include all the current values that are aligned with your vision as well as the newly identified values, and prioritize them to enable you to realize your vision. See the example below.

Current Values	Vision Aligned	New Values	Prioritized Values
Security	Y/N	Adventure	Authenticity
Authenticity	Y/N		Adventure
	Y/N		
	Y/N		
	Y/N		
	Y/N		
	Y/N		
	Y/N		
	Y/N		
	Y/N		

After you have completed the exercise, reflect on the changes you need to make. Did you identify any values that were not supportive of your vision and need to be de-prioritized or dropped off your list? Did you re-prioritize some of your values based on your vision? If you have made changes to your values or their prioritization, it's good practice to review the decisions you are making by examining your new values, although applying them will take some work and getting used to.

THE ACTION PLAN

You may have heard the saying "Energy flows where the attention goes." When we focus on something, it expands. It's so hard these days to keep our attention where we want it—what with social media, email, podcasts, being available for work 24/7, and always being connected. But it's clear that the mind works a lot better when it's focused; we need focus to develop our action plan, through which we can convert our dreams, our change plan, into reality!

One challenge with converting our vision into an action plan is that the work to achieve this creates such a huge to-do list that our brain gets overloaded and depressed just from looking at it. The trick is to focus on actions for six months at a time.

Identify Your Change Priorities

As a starting point for creating your action plan, refer back to the change plan you created in Step 4. Identify the priorities you wanted to focus on in the short-term based on the areas with the biggest gap between your current and desired scores. Make sure that this prioritization based on your gap scores feels right—the areas with the biggest gaps aren't necessarily the most important ones to work on. Also use your gut to prioritize the areas: What's important to you now? What do you want to work on first? What will give you the biggest "bang for your buck" if you start working on it today?

After you've chosen your areas of focus, write them down on the Action Plan Worksheet. You can find a template at http://www.authentes.com/finding-your-rhythm.

Look Six Months Ahead

Now you are almost ready to convert this information into concrete actions. But before you do, answer this question: What would success look like for you in six months?

For example, if you want to work on improving your social life, your six-month goal could be that you want to have participated in nine social events and have three people you now regularly connect with. Or if you want to work on your physical fitness, your goal could be to have joined a gym, increased your muscle mass by 12 percent, and decreased your fat by 20 percent. Make your vision tangible. The reason for defining success in six-month increments is so that you can measure at that time whether you are on the right track.

Let me give you another example. Imagine you recently participated in an intensive coach-training program. You loved it. In fact, you loved it so much that you envision yourself quitting your job and becoming an executive coach. You have the qualifications and a lot of business experience, but not the coaching experience yet. For you, success in six months could be having coached ten clients for ten hours each. Creating this six-month vision of success for yourself will help you determine which actions you need to take to get there.

Determine Action Items

The next step is to list your action items—the concrete steps you need to take to reach your goal in six months. Include at least one action item for each of those six months. Of course, they might change once you start working on them, but it's important to map out a reasonable, achievable plan to hold yourself accountable. (Try not to get too attached to the schedule; be flexible with however your success unfolds.)

Do not include actions that are too vague, such as "Coach two clients." No, make sure the actions are concrete. If your goal is to have one hundred hours of coaching experience in six months, how will you achieve that? Where will you get your clients? Your action items might include the following:

- Make a deal with my boss to work four days a week rather than five in the next six months
- Prepare a list of events where I can meet potential clients
- Send a message to my network through social media to make them aware of my coaching skills
- Develop a standard coaching agreement that I can use with my clients

As you can see, these moves are all measurable. You want to make sure that your measurement of success is s-t-r-e-t-c-h-e-d, but not unattainable.

Review Your Action Plan

After you have written down your actions for the next six months, take a step back and assess whether they will get you to the success you wanted to create in that period.

Although action planning may sound easy, it's typically the hardest part of the process for my clients. Just getting to the point where you can start action planning takes a lot of energy. The Finding Your Rhythm process can be fun at first, because you can start dreaming about what you would like your life to look like, without having to put in the work, but the action-planning stage is where the rubber hits the road. In this phase, you have to commit to taking the concrete steps needed to realize your vision. You must decide what you are going to do and when. This is why the review at the end is so important: you need to make sure that the actions will get you to your six-month goal. In order to do that, they need to be detailed and actionable and have your full commitment.

Share Your Action Plan

The most important part of action planning is the one most people skip: sharing your action plan. That's right, invite someone (or a group of people—maybe your personal board of directors, as discussed in Step 4) to give you feedback. It can be tough to have someone review your plan, but it's a terrific way to ensure that your plan is robust and complete. This person or group can also help you stay focused on the plan's execution. Next we'll discuss ways to spread the word about your vision.

SHARING YOUR VISION

A number of years ago, I was having lunch with the founder of an NGO that was supporting African artists. He had set up an amazing crowd-funding platform and was having great success exposing these artists to a global audience. When I asked him how he had come up with the idea and how long he had worked on putting his vision into action, he told me the following story.

> "I have always been inspired by music. I travel around the world, and I always try to get a feel for the local music scene. A few years ago, I visited Africa and was so inspired by the amazing music I heard in all the places I visited. I loved the artists' passion for music and was awed by the quality of many of the performances. I started asking myself why these artists were only known in their small towns. It almost felt like a crime that this music could not be shared with the world. And that's how I came up with the idea. As soon as I got home, I started writing a vision and a business plan. I created a website, a logo, and a business card, and made a database of all the artists I had seen and wanted to stay connected to. I worked on this for months. I had a day job as a manager at a global oil company, but every evening I was working on my idea. The problem was that the idea was not leaving my room.
>
> "I got promoted at my company, and as a result I was asked to participate in a weeklong leadership development program. At the end of the week, we were all sitting in a circle and the facilitator asked the following question: 'What are you going to do differently once you walk out of this door?' I became really anxious. I knew what I wanted to do differently, but I also knew that it was not the politically correct answer. People started sharing things like building better

relationships with stakeholders, being more focused on the customer, being more results oriented, etcetera. I had made up something I was going to say about creating a more innovative company culture, but when it was my turn, I couldn't say it. Instead I stood up and said, 'I'm going to quit my job and build an NGO that opens up a global audience to African artists.' You can imagine the looks I got. But for me, that was the moment when it all happened. I shared my story, and at that point there was no way back!"

This was an important lesson for me. Many of my clients have admitted to creating business plans, websites, and business cards that never made it to reality. They stayed in a dreamscape. Why? Accountability. If you are the only one privy to your plan, it is very easy to tell yourself that something is an interesting idea and then immediately talk yourself out of it. But once you start sharing your plan with others, you become accountable to them. You become much more committed to making your vision a reality.

Sharing your vision is casting the dice so the vision can start attracting the energy that will propel you toward making it a reality. When my then-partner and I were setting up a foundation, we got very excited about the things we were going to do. Once we shared our plans with the people around us, it was amazing how many of them offered to support us through funding or other services. People offered to build our website, do all the legal paperwork, pay for the flights to India where we were doing our first project, and so forth. It was incredible to see how our positive energy attracted so much support!

This was a long introduction to what I believe should be the number one item on your action plan: Share your vision! Don't keep it to yourself. Discuss your vision with the people you meet; show them how much passion you have for it. You'll quickly discover that your passion is contagious!

KEEPING THE BEAT GOING

The Finding Your Rhythm process does not end when you make your action plan. It keeps repeating itself. Once you've made your plan and started executing it, there will come a time when you'll need to stop, reflect, and make sure that you're still listening to your rhythm and that it's still in sync with your vision for your life.

Once you have been through the whole process, the follow-up processes take a lot less time but involve the same steps. In a typical coaching engagement I have regular biweekly sessions with my clients for a period of four to six months, during which we walk through the various steps of the Finding Your Rhythm process. After that, it's up to the client to start executing the action plan. Subsequently, I typically check in monthly to see whether my client is still on track with the plan.

If you do not work with a coach, make sure that you set a very clear check-in time for yourself. Block out time during a specific day on your calendar during which you would like to reflect on where you are with your plan. As we discussed, having a coach, friend, or personal board of directors helps! But if no one else is there to hold you accountable, make sure you're honest with yourself: don't mark things off as done when you still have work to do.

We all have moments when we feel demotivated. Maybe planned actions turn out to be harder than we thought, or we're too busy to give the actions much attention. That's to be expected; it happens to everyone. Try breaking down your action items into smaller, more doable steps. Or go back to basics by reevaluating your priorities and making time for the things that matter most. You should also revisit your vision board or the vision you wrote down. Rebooting a visioning practice, if yours fell by the wayside, can help you recapture the feeling of living the life you've envisioned. It can also be a good motivator to start putting in the extra time needed to put the vision into action!

CELEBRATING

And now for the fun part: the celebration! The good news about the celebration is that it does not have to wait until you've achieved your goal. Obviously when you do achieve it, when you get the email that one million copies of your book have been sold, or when you get hired for the job you always wanted, celebrate! But it also really helps to start celebrating your achievements as you work toward your goal.

One of my clients, Laurain, felt as though she had nothing to celebrate after months of working on her action plan. Let's look at how a shift in her perspective gave her lots to be proud of.

Laurain: Karel, I have been in my role for one year now, and I haven't made any progress. When I look at the organization today, we still aren't ahead of the competition, we still don't collaborate in a way that helps us create more value, and we still are too focused on financial results. I don't know what to do. Maybe it's just me. Maybe I'm the wrong person for the job.

Me: Laurain, would you allow me to go back a year?

Laurain: Sure.

Me: Do you remember the session we did after you had been in your role for three months? The session when you created your vision, determined your main priorities, and developed the action plan to make it all happen? Just remind me, what was the organization like when you started in your role?

Laurain: Mmmm . . . We were on the verge of falling over. We hardly had enough cash to pay salaries and our vendors. We had no clear vision, and a lot of talented people were giving up and leaving the firm. We were definitely not in a good space, but I knew that when I took over. And in my gut, I knew there was a lot of potential in the company, from both an economic and a social perspective.

Me: Yes, that was a totally different situation than today. Just looking back at my notes from that session, you identified the following priorities:

1.   improve financial position
2.   develop a strong leadership team

3. develop and communicate my vision for the company
4. build trusted relationships with our customers
5. build a culture of trust, collaboration, and passion

You also had a clear view of what success would look like after one year. If you reflect on those priorities, how successful have you been in achieving the goals you set for yourself?

Laurain: [*Silence*] Yes. I guess if you look at it from that perspective, I did come a long way. Although we still aren't performing at the same level as our competition if you look at our financial benchmarks, we are in a position now where we don't have to worry about paying our people and our vendors. I have made changes in the leadership team, and I am very happy with how we're working together on the vision that we further developed as a team. Our customer satisfaction score is up significantly, and we're starting to see a number of really strong relationships developing. And I am also happy to say that our employee engagement score has improved from four to six-point-five on a scale from one to ten. So, still a lot of work to do, but if I reflect on where we are compared to last year, I should actually be opening the champagne tonight!

This amnesia about progress happens a lot. We get so focused on the elements that still need improvement or change that we forget to look back at the successes we've had so far. So when you think about awareness in a time of change, remember to be aware of all the changes you're making, all the small steps you're taking, and make the time to reflect on the many steps you've already taken on the path to your vision. Small achievements build momentum!

Why celebrate? Celebrating makes us pause and think about our accomplishments. It makes us mindful of the moment. And according to Fred Bryant and Joseph Veroff, authors of *Savoring: A New Model of Positive Experience*,[74] when we stop to savor the good stuff, we buffer ourselves against the bad and build resilience; even minicelebrations can activate positive emotions that help us manage the stress from daily challenges.

Precelebrations

There are many ways to celebrate, including what I call precelebration. This is when you celebrate the vision or goal you are going to achieve in the future. As part of my visioning workshops, I've created an exercise called Celebrating the Future to do just that. I start this exercise by bringing in a bottle of champagne (with or without alcohol, depending on the audience) and glasses. Next I ask participants to think about this group five years from now. I ask them to imagine that they have realized their visions and achieved the goals they set for themselves. After five minutes of envisioning this, I ask everyone to gather around and pretend we are in that moment—five years from now, on a beautiful beach, celebrating the success of their venture. One by one, each person makes a toast and highlights what makes them so proud to be there today. As you might imagine, the toasts can be very inspirational and motivating. Here are some of the most memorable:

- "Remember that day in Bangkok when we did that vision workshop? We wanted to have an impact on the lives of one million small farmers by helping them create a steady income. We thought it would be a stretch, but by working together as a team and keeping this vision in mind with every decision we made, we did it. I am so proud to be part of this amazing team!"
- "I would have never thought that our vision would have such a tremendous impact on our people's engagement. By following through on our vision as a leadership team, we have also won the trust of our employees, and it is so fantastic to see our employee engagement scores consistently at almost perfect levels!"
- "We had to fight to get here. But man was it worth it. It has been an amazing journey and I would not have wanted to do this with any other team!"

People really experience how it feels to be in that moment. And the more toasts that are made, the more enthusiastic they get. It is always fantastic to see people walk out of the workshop full of energy and with a positive attitude toward realizing the vision.

Minicelebrations

"Minicelebrations" are another way to observe and appreciate what you've accomplished so far. These start with awareness—with taking the time to notice moments of achievement, however minor.

When I shared Laurain's story with another of my clients, he took the message very seriously. He went so far as to put a Post-it Note on his car's rearview mirror that read, "What am I proud of today?" He knew that every day when he got home and reversed into his parking spot, he would look in the mirror and reflect on that question.

The thing you're proud of that day could be small. Maybe you offered a stranger a compliment that made them smile, or you made time to talk to one of your employees who was going through a challenging time, or you finished the next chapter of your book, or you exercised or signed up for a meditation retreat. There are many accomplishments to celebrate!

Another aspect of minicelebrations is stepping out of your normal routine. At home this could mean going to a special place—a bench in the garden, or a room where you normally meditate. Just making the time to reflect on what you have achieved is a good way to "minicelebrate." At work it could mean taking a break and going somewhere to celebrate with the relevant group of people.

When you do celebrate, make it a moment. Raise a toast, say a prayer, sing a song, dance. Do something to really make that moment stick. The more you do this, the more positive energy you create.

The Real Thing

Of course, when you do achieve your goal, there should be a huge celebration. I have many times seen leaders celebrate as follows: "This has been a fantastic year. We beat our target by 50 percent! We should be proud of ourselves! So let's discuss how we can beat the target again next year!" This is not celebrating. Of course it is great that at least the achievement is mentioned, but stepping over the achievement and immediately turning it into the target for next year will create more anxiety than a sense of accomplishment.

In my professional career I have experienced various ways of celebrating, and a lot were like the noncelebration I just mentioned. However, there were also leaders who really understood how to do it. One of the people I had the honor to get to know was the CEO of a consulting firm in the Netherlands. To celebrate the growth and progress of his company, he would take all of his approximately 150 employees on a journey every year, from a trip to India to participate in a yoga retreat, to a trip to Washington, DC, to attend the inauguration of President Obama. Of course not everyone is in a position to organize trips and celebrate success like this. Some other suggestions are camping with the whole team, including spouses and kids, or go skiing together for a weekend. The possibilities are endless, and the celebration will have an enormous positive impact if the leader who organizes it is doing this from their heart—in other words, when the leader celebrates with the team to authentically thank them for all their achievements.

KEY BEATS

In this chapter, we took the fifth and final step of the Finding Your Rhythm journey: Play! Creating an action plan is the culmination of all your hard work, and it's what's going to drive your success. In this step, we discussed these main ideas:

- You must upgrade your beliefs to support yourself in reaching your goals.
- Reviewing your values and prioritizing them gives you structure and direction for achieving your goals.
- Creating an action plan is paramount! You must also share your vision and action plan so that you are held accountable for implementing them.
- Celebrating our achievements is worthwhile—and fun!

ENJOY YOUR RHYTHM

A number of years ago, I heard a story about the CEO of a company that specialized in cat and dog food. The company's mission was "to improve the lives of cats and dogs." Needless to say, the CEO was an animal lover and so was his leadership team. And because of their passion for pets, their activities started expanding to other areas of companion-animal wellness, such as supporting animal shelters. This passion also paid off, and financially they were very successful. The company was so successful that one day, the CEO received a phone call asking if he'd be interviewed for the cover story for an upcoming issue of *Forbes* magazine. He declined. People around him were flabbergasted—why did he decline? He replied, "I do not see how me being on the cover of *Forbes* is going to improve the lives of cats and dogs."

Stay True to Your Rhythm

NOTES

1   John F. Helliwell et al. *World Happiness Report* 2021. 2021. New York: Sustainable Development Solutions Network.

2   *Webster's Revised Unabridged Dictionary.* 1913. C & G Merriam Co.

3   Aniruddh D. Patel and John R. Iversen. "The Evolutionary Neuroscience of Musical Beat Perception: The Action Simulation for Auditory Prediction (ASAP) Hypothesis." 2014. *Frontiers in Systems Neuroscience.* https://www.ncbi.nlm.nih.gov/pmc/articles/PMC4026735/.

4   Joseph Jordania. *Time to Fight and Time to Relax: Singing and Humming at the Beginnings of Human Evolutionary History.* 2009. Kadmos.

5   Givewell Munyaradzi and Webster Zimidzi. "Comparison of Western Music and African Music." 2012. *Creative Education* 3, no. 2: 193–195.

6   "Traditional Work Songs." Library of Congress Celebrates the Songs of America. Library of Congress. https://www.loc.gov/collections/songs-of-america/articles-and-essays/musical-styles/traditional-and-ethnic/traditional-work-songs/.

7   Ed Christman. "Iggy Pop Opens a 'Window into the Soul' on Virgin's Contemplative 'Avenue B.'" 1999. *Billboard* 111: 14.

8   Patrick E. Savage. *Cultural Evolution of Music.* 2019. Palgrave Communications, 5, 16.

9   Christina Nombela et al. "Into the Groove: Can Rhythm Influence Parkinson's Disease?" pt. 2. 2013. *Neuroscience & Biobehavioral Reviews* 37, no. 10.

10   Massimiliano Pau et al. "Effects of Physical Rehabilitation Integrated with Rhythmic Auditory Stimulation on Spatio-Temporal and Kinematic Parameters of Gait in Parkinson's Disease." 2016. *Frontiers in Neurology* 7:126.

11   Sanjay Gupta, MD. *Keep Sharp: Build a Better Brain at Any Age.* 2021. Simon & Schuster.

12   George A. Miller. "The Magic Number Seven, Plus or Minus Two: Some

Limits on Our Capacity for Processing Information." 1956. *Psychological Review* 63: 81–93.

13   Ardon Shorr. *Unlocking Music with Neuroscience.* TEDx Talk. 2012. https://www.youtube.com/watch?v=cswhOCKQZ7Q.

14   Gaia staff. *Mysteries of the Human Heart.* 2020. https://www.gaia.com.

15   Julie Tseng and Jordan Poppenk. "Brain Meta-State Transitions Demarcate Thoughts across Task Contexts Exposing the Mental Noise of Trait Neuroticism." 2020. *Nature Communications* 11, article 3480.

16   Amrisha Vaish, Tobias Grossmann, and Amanda Woodward. "Not All Emotions Are Created Equal: The Negativity Bias in Social-Emotional Development." 2008. *Psychological Bulletin* 134, no. 3: 383–403.

17   Kendra Cherry. *What Is the Negativity Bias?* 2020. https://www.ver ywellmind.com/negative-bias-4589618.

18   Michael Lewis and Jeanne Brooks-Gunn. "Individual Differences in Visual Self-Recognition as a Function of Mother-Infant Attachment Relationship." 1985. *Developmental Psychology* 21, no. 6: 1181–87.

19   Matthew A. Killingsworth and Daniel T. Gilbert. "A Wandering Mind Is an Unhappy Mind." 2010. *Science* 330.

20   Hermann Hesse. *Siddhartha.* 1922. New Directions.

21   Kaushal Patel. *Types of Meditation.* https://www.slideshare.net /KaushalPatel41/types-of-meditation-51763102.

22   Ananda Balayogi Bhavanani. "Yoga: The Ideal Way of Life." 2013. *Yoga Mimamsa* 44, no. 4:314–25.

23   Chris Cowley and Henry S. Lodge, MD. *Younger Next Year: Live Strong, Fit, and Sexy—Until You're 80 and Beyond.* 2007. Workman Publishing Company.

24   Heinrich Klüver and Paul Bucy. "'Psychic Blindness' and Other Symptoms Following Bilateral Temporal Lobectomy in Rhesus Monkeys." 1937. *American Journal of Physiology* 119: 352–53.

25   John Watson and Rosalie Rayner. "Conditioned Emotional Reactions." 1920. *Journal of Experimental Psychology* 3: 1–14.

26   Jared B. Torre and Matthew D. Lieberman. "Putting Feelings into Words: Affect Labeling as Implicit Emotion Regulation." 2018. *Emotion Review* 10, no. 2: 116–24.

27   Killingsworth and Gilbert. "A Wandering Mind."

28   Moshe Bensimon, Dorit Amir, and Yuval Wolf. "Drumming Through Trauma: Music Therapy with Post-Traumatic Soldiers." 2008. *The Arts in Psychotherapy* 35, no. 1: 34–48.

29   Jochim Hansen. "What You Hear Shapes How You Think: Sound Patterns Change Level of Construal." 2014. *Journal of Experimental Social Psychology* 54: 131–38.

30   Cormac Larkin. "Music Activates the Brain at a High Level." Interview with Melody Gardot. 2016. *Irish Times.*

31 Catherine Ward Thompson et al. "More Green Space Is Linked to Less Stress in Deprived Communities: Evidence from Salivary Cortisol Patterns." 2011. *Landscape and Urban Planning* 105, no. 3: 221–29.

32 Ming Kuo, Rebekah Levine Coley, and William C. Sullivan. "Where Does Community Grow? The Social Context Created by Nature in Urban Public Housing." 1997. *Environment and Behavior* 29, no. 4: 468–94.

33 Gia Marson. "Spending Time in Nature Can Be Good for Your Mental Health." 2021. https://drgiamarson.com/spending-time-in-nature -can-be-good-for-your-mental-health/.

34 Stephen T. Garnett et al. "A Spatial Overview of the Global Importance of Indigenous Lands for Conservation." 2018. *Nature Sustainability* 1: 369–74.

35 Nina Wegner. "How Indigenous Cultures Can Save the Modern World." 2012. https://www.huffpost.com/entry/how-indigenous-cultures -c_b_1234915.

36 Y. Miyazaki, T. Morikawa, and E. Hatakeyama. "Nature and Comfort." *Proceeding of 6th International Congress of Physiological Anthropology.* 2002.

37 Mathew P. White et al. "Spending at Least 120 Minutes a Week in Nature Is Associated with Good Health and Wellbeing." 2019. *Scientific Reports* 9: 7730.

38 Qing Li et al. "Effects of Forest Bathing on Cardiovascular and Metabolic Parameters in Middle-Aged Males." 2014. *Evidence Based Complement Alternative Medicine.* https://www.researchgate.net /publication/305339887_Effects_of_Forest_Bathing_on_Cardiovascular _and_Metabolic_Parameters_in_Middle-Aged_Males.

39 Hermann Graf von Keyserling. *The Travel Diary of a Philosopher.* 1919. Harcourt.

40 Melissa A. Leath. *Does Your Child See Sparkles? Help for Parents Guiding Psychic Kids.* 2013. CreateSpace.

41 Thomas Freese. "Kids See Ghosts." 2013. https://www.literacyworldwide .org/blog/literacy-now/2013/10/31/kids-see-ghosts.

42 Shahram Shiva. "Ego Is Good." 2015. https://www.huffpost.com/entry /ego-is-good_b_7641706.

43 Johann Hari. *Lost Connections: Why You're Depressed and How to Find Hope.* 2018. Bloomsbury Publishing.

44 Anthony D. Ong et al. "Emodiversity and Biomarkers of Inflammation." 2018. *Emotion* 18, no. 1: 3–14.

45 Jason Marsh and Vicki Zakrzewski. "Four Lessons from 'Inside Out' to Discuss with Kids." 2015. https://greatergood.berkeley.edu/article/item /four_lessons_from_inside_out_to_discuss_with_kids.

46 June Gruber, Iris B. Mauss, and Maya Tamir. "A Dark Side of Happiness? How, When, and Why Happiness Is Not Always Good." 2011. *Perspectives on Psychological Science* 6: 222.

47 Nathaniel F. Watson et al. "Recommended Amount of Sleep for a Healthy Adult: A Joint Consensus Statement of the American Academy of Sleep Medicine and Sleep Research Society." 2015. *Sleep* 38, no. 6.

48 Jim Sollisch. "Multitasking Makes Us a Little Dumber." August 10, 2010. *Chicago Tribune.*

49 Amy Muise, Ulrich Schimmack, and Emily A. Impett. "Sexual Frequency Predicts Greater Well-Being, But More Is Not Always Better." 2015. *Social Psychological and Personality Science* 7, no. 4.

50 Sheri Stritof. "The Benefits of Having Sex More Often: Emotional, Physical, and Relationship Benefits of Frequent Sex." 2019. https://www .verywellmind.com/why-should-you-have-sex-more-often-2300937.

51 Shellie R. Warren. "10 Most Common Reasons for Divorce." 2021. https://www.marriage.com/advice/divorce/10-most-common -reasons-for-divorce/.

52 Kirsty L. Spalding et al. "Retrospective Birth Dating of Cells in Humans." 2005. *Cell* 122: 133–43.

53 https://gamechangersmovie.com.

54 Jim Clifton. "The World's Broken Workplace." June 13, 2017. Gallup, The Chairman's Blog. https://news.gallup.com/opinion/chairman/212045 /world-broken-workplace.aspx.

55 Andrew T. Jebb et al. "Happiness, Income Satiation and Turning Points Around the World." 2018. *Nature Human Behaviour* 2: 33–38.

56 Marie Kondo. *The Life-Changing Magic of Tidying Up: The Japanese Art of Decluttering and Organizing.* 2015. Berkeley: Ten Speed Press.

57 "Pre-Hire Assessments: 10 Compelling Reasons Pre-Hire Assessments Boost Your Hiring Process." https://assessment.aon.com/en-us /solutions/pre-hire-assessment.

58 Akira Sakamoto. "Popular Psychological Tests and Self-Fulfilling Prophecy." 2000. *Asian Journal of Social Psychology.*

59 Mark Manson. "7 Strange Questions That Help You Find Your Life Purpose." https://markmanson.net/life-purpose.

60 Malcolm Gladwell. *Outliers.* 2011. Back Bay Books.

61 A. Pascal-Leone et al. "Modulation of Muscle Responses Evoked by Transcranial Magnetic Stimulation During the Acquisition of New Fine Motor Skills." 1995. *Journal of Neurophysiology* 74, no. 3: 1037–45.

62 Neville Goddard. *At Your Command.* 1939. TarcherPerigee.

63 For more information, listen to the Buddhism and Science lectures by Graham Priest. https://www.youtube.com/watch?v=V-P3j3S2beA.

64 Joe Vitale. *How to Manifest Miracles: The Miracle 6 Steps to Enlightenment.* 2017. https://www.youtube.com/watch?v=dzSxexrBUFA.

65 Charles Duhigg. *The Power of Habit: Why We Do What We Do in Life and Business.* 2014. Random House.

66 David T. Neal, Wendy Wood, and Jeffrey M. Quinn. "Habits: A Repeat Performance." 2006. *Current Directions in Psychological Science* 15, no. 4: 198–202.

67 Robert M. Yerkes and John D. Dodson. "The Relation of Strength and Stimulus to Rapidity of Habit-Formation." 1908. *Journal of Comparative Neurology and Psychology* 18: 459–82.

68 Eva M. Krockow. "Is It Time to Step Outside Your Comfort Zone?" August 23, 2019. https://www.psychologytoday.com/us/blog/stretching -theory/201908/is-it-time-step-outside-your-comfort-zone.

69 Shi Heng Yi. *5 Hindrances to Self-Mastery.* TEDx Talk. 2020. https://www.youtube.com/watch?v=4-079YIasck.

70 Bill Plotkin. *Wild Mind.* 2013. New World Library.

71 Bronnie Ware. *The Top Five Regrets of the Dying.* 2012. Hay House.

72 Byron Katie. *Loving What Is: Four Questions That Can Change Your Life.* 2002. Crown Archetype.

73 Tony Robbins. *Awaken the Giant Within.* 1992. Simon & Schuster.

74 Fred B. Bryant and Joseph Veroff. *Savoring: A New Model of Positive Experience.* 2006. Psychology Press.

ABOUT THE AUTHOR

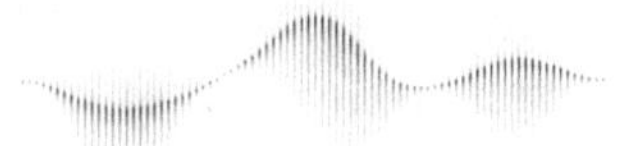

"Inspiring leaders to create meaningful breakthroughs."

Karel Bakkes is an executive coach with a proven track record of using his business development and consulting skills to deliver results. He has worked with clients and partners in more than fifty countries. His clients have included C-suite and senior executives who were transitioning into new roles, managers stuck in their jobs, and people who were generally stuck in their lives. He helped them *find their rhythm.*

After a short career in music, Karel moved into the corporate world and studied economics and auditing. He was a partner in a Big Four firm for many years and held many different executive leadership positions in various countries, including the Netherlands, the United States, Belgium, China, New Zealand, and most recently Thailand. In the latter part of his Big Four career, Karel was leading the relationship with a number of global clients.

His passion for coaching was always the building block of his success, whether it was leading a nonperforming office through a transformation, building up a relationship with a large client, starting new teams, or helping client executives transition into new roles or challenges.

Karel is the founder and CEO of Authentes, a company dedicated to his life purpose of "inspiring leaders to create meaningful breakthroughs." With clients across the globe, Karel is now supporting many executives and their teams in realizing their visions.